Neil Ansell is an award-winning television journalist and a long-standing writer for the broadsheets. He is the author of two previous books, *Deep Country* and *Deer Island*, and has contributed to nature programmes and wildlife documentaries, though his main focus was news and current affairs. He has two daughters and lives in Brighton.

Praise for *The Last Wilderness*:

'*The Last Wilderness* is a moving and mesmerising book. Ansell's quiet, respectful immersion in the landscape rewards with some startling encounters with the natural world. He is a knowledgeable and generous guide to the unique flora and fauna of this beautiful corner of Scotland' James Macdonald Lockhart, author of RAPTOR

'[A] captivating memoir . . . vivid as photographs, yet sketched with something more profound than simple reportage. Beneath the measured, knowledgeable, unfussy voice is a meaningful, and even important record: not just of a changing landscape, but of a man such places have shaped' *The Herald*

'Beautiful . . . a testimony to reticent courage' *Daily Mail*

'Lyrical, thought-provoking' *Scotsman*

'Neil Ansell is a genuine creature of the wild. His knowledge of remote places, and his love for them, come from deep and sustained immersion. He writes in prose which is entirely right for its subject – unshowy, level-headed, quietly surprising. *The Last Wilderness* is a wonderful experience which tingles with all the sensations of being out on the hill, in all weathers, alone' Philip Marsden, author of RISING GROUND

'Ansell has the rare skill of combining vividly the intimacy of detail and the astonishing grandeur of this North West coastline of Scotland. Through his keen eyes we look again at the familiar with a sense of wondrous revelation' Madeleine Bunting, author of LOVE OF COUNTRY

'Beautifully charts the challenges and solaces of being alone and part of nature' *Bookseller*

'A beautifully written account of the author's journeys to some of the most remote parts of Britain in search of solitude and solace' *Choice*

'A love letter to Scotland . . . how I wish I could go back to Arisaig and the Small Isles. How much I missed, but how glad I am to experience it now with this wonderful writer' *My Weekly*

'*The Last Wilderness* is a beautiful read; rich in descriptive detail . . . his passion for the environment and his sublime prose make it a book to be savoured' *CultureFly*

'A hauntingly beautiful memoir on nature, solitude and hearing loss' Waterstones.com

'He captures the landscape and the sense of adventure exquisitely: enough to make me feel I've been there but leaving me longing to make a trek of my own' *The Pool*

'[A] haunting, lyrical memoir' *Simple Things*

NEIL ANSELL

THE LAST WILDERNESS

A JOURNEY INTO SILENCE

TINDER
PRESS

First published in Great Britain in 2018 by Tinder Press
An imprint of HEADLINE PUBLISHING GROUP

First published in this paperback edition in 2018 by Tinder Press
An imprint of HEADLINE PUBLISHING GROUP

8

Cataloguing in Publication Data is available from the British Library

ISBN 978 1 4722 4712 4

Typeset in Scala by Avon DataSet Ltd, Bidford-on-Avon, Warwickshire

Printed and bound in Great Britain by Clays Ltd, Elcograf S.p.A.

HEADLINE PUBLISHING GROUP
An Hachette UK Company
Carmelite House
50 Victoria Embankment
London EC4Y 0DZ

www.tinderpress.co.uk
www.headline.co.uk
www.hachette.co.uk

Contents

PREFACE

The Rough Bounds

The Rough Bounds of Lochaber, *Na Garbh Chriochan*, form a part of the North-West Highlands of Scotland so named for their remoteness and inaccessibility, their sense of being a place apart. On this far western shore rugged peninsulas reach out into the Atlantic like the fingers of an outstretched hand, each one pointing out to the islands. They are indented by long deep sea-lochs and cut off from the mainland by a chain of bare snow-capped mountains. Knoydart, the largest and northernmost of these peninsulas, the thumb of this supplicant hand, is notorious for having no road access whatsoever and has been dubbed Britain's last great wilderness, though this is to draw a veil over its long history of settlement by crofters, of emigration, of forced clearances. Yet in a world where the air that we breathe and the waters that surround us are all contaminated by our activities, nowhere is untouched, and wildness is relative. A place can only appear to be less touched than others.

My first visit to the area was a lifetime ago, and when I first came to the Highlands it was the wildest landscape I had ever seen. This was the beginning, for me, of years of travel, and in particular of seeking out the world's wild places, whether that be the frozen wastes beyond the Arctic Circle or the sand dunes of the Sahara, climbing mountains to where rivers first sprang from the foot of a crumbling glacier or gazing down into the molten heart of an active volcano.

There were occasions when I travelled with a companion, but as time went on I became more and more drawn to life as a solitary wanderer, and the freedom to follow my whims without discussion or compromise. It sometimes feels that I am designed for solitude. I don't believe myself to be in any way antisocial, it is just that company has become something that I feel I can manage perfectly well without. The truth is that when I am on my own I never seem to feel I'm missing anything; I'm at ease with my own company. It's not only for psychological reasons that I consider myself particularly suited for life as something of a loner, but for practical reasons also. I have been deaf in one ear since infancy, and the hearing in what I call my 'good' ear is severely compromised too, and is rapidly deteriorating. It has left me feeling semi-detached, as if everyone else is away in another room, beyond a wall of silence.

I wonder sometimes just how much this might have affected my life choices. It was never quite severe enough for me to be sent to a special school where I could learn sign language and keep company with others with hearing difficulties. Rather, I was left to struggle on as best I could in regular school. In a one-to-one situation I manage pretty well; I position myself carefully, I hear a bit, lip-read a bit, and guess a bit, and I have had a lifetime's practice at muddling along this way, so that oftentimes people I meet will never even guess that I am basically winging it. But put me in a group of people, all talking, or in an environment where there is a background noise, and I am quickly lost, and will soon find myself drifting off to the periphery, into a private silence. Perhaps this has been why I have always been drawn to solitary activities since early childhood, my head in a book or alone on a country walk, indulging my fascination for the natural world. Or indeed, becoming a writer, where I can communicate by means of the written word rather than conversation. It is simply easier that way, free of the frustrations of having to engage socially. It makes me feel a little apart from things, my head in a box, with everything muffled and dreamlike; a keen observer rather than a participant. It sometimes feels that I am only loosely tethered to the world.

After years of travel and rootlessness, I settled in the mountains of mid-Wales, living alone in a cottage with no services whatsoever, growing my own food, foraging, and watching the birds. My world reduced to contain only what was in daily walking distance. And so, after five years of roaming, I spent five years learning how to stay still. Each of these two ways of seeing the world – the restless and the rooted – has its own unique virtues. When I am on the move, and seeing things for the first time, the shock of the new gives me an intensity of experience, a sudden depth of focus that will perhaps never be replicated. When I stay in one place I become gradually aware of how things are more subtle and complex than they first appeared, of how malleable and mutable is the world, of how it fluxes and changes with the seasons and the passage of time.

My life in more recent years has been on the face of it

more conventional; living in a flat by the sea with my two daughters, and writing about the world as much as living in it. When I was a young man, my travels were freewheeling, open-ended. I would take to the road with no particular destination in mind, seeking work where I could find it, and might not return for weeks, or months, or even years. This is no longer possible for me; not since having children. I have no complaints, for it is part of the contract you make when you choose to become a parent; you accept that your life is no longer entirely your own. Now my children are growing up, I can begin to feel my horizons opening up once again. I have obligations, so I can't just take off as I once would have, but with forethought I can at least dip a toe into the waters of freedom.

And so I came up with a plan. I wanted to achieve a synthesis between the intensity of the new that comes with first sight, and the depth that comes with familiarity, by choosing a place that was relatively accessible and returning again and again, in all weathers and in every season. Rather than looking back on the entire journey and creating a narrative out of it retrospectively, I liked the idea of writing up each leg of the journey, noting my observations, thoughts and reflections, before I embarked on the next leg. Part of the very essence of travel is uncertainty, not knowing where it will lead you next. Writing as I went would be more like the journey itself, more like life. Travel takes you to places that you could never have quite imagined, not in detail, not in their singularity, and it may also lead you to unexpected corners of your own self.

I chose these barely remembered hills of the Rough Bounds, because that is where it all began for me; it was my first experience of wilderness, or the appearance of it. I had always thought that I would return one day to get to know the place a little better, and I am running out of time. I pictured myself heading out into the most remote fastnesses of these far hills, camping alone and far from human habitation, and in doing so finding my own rough bounds, my own outer limits. It is a part of the story that I tell myself about who I am. I have an assumption that I shall once again find myself alone on a mountainside, and that to me, and to others who feel the same way, this is an essential part of what makes life worth living.

This book is based around five visits spread over the

course of a year, each consisting of about a week of solitary walking and reflection. I had no planned route, and no final destination in mind. It will not serve as any kind of guidebook to the area, for it is partial and impressionistic, just a walk in the wilds, a meditation on nature and an exploration of memory and desire. This had seemed like a very modest ambition, a relaxed and manageable return to the wandering life for someone who had been to many of the wildest and most far-flung corners of the earth. Yet as the year wore on and I penetrated deeper and deeper into these wilds my health began to fail me, and it turned out to be far more of a physical and mental challenge than I had ever anticipated.

NOVEMBER

Still Waters

A heron was standing frozen at the water's edge, gunmetal grey and steely-eyed, poised over the drifting kelp. There was a penetrating fine rain falling, hardly more than a mist, and all was still, as if paused. The hills across the loch, only a few hundred yards distant, were barely visible through the smirr, just a shadow of themselves. Though this was a sea-loch, a fjord by another name, here was twenty miles inland from the open ocean. There was no trace of a wave on its surface; the waters were so smooth and unmarked they seemed stretched, swollen like the skin of a balloon. It felt as though a single jab of the heron's bill and the whole scene would burst apart.

If it had not been so profoundly calm I probably would not have noticed the unexpected ripple far out on the water. Though with no reference points it is hard to judge size and distance, I knew at once that it was an otter. A rising seal will tip its head back as if it is looking at the sky, while an otter will rest its head flat along the surface of the water. A seal will float vertically, an otter horizontally. It was in full hunting mode, diving and surfacing repeatedly. It did not just sink into the water; it would give a little leap to propel itself downward. First its head would rise, and then swivel downwards, and so it would coil itself into the water, its back the arc of a circle. Sometimes it would flick up its tail, so that this would point straight up for a moment before sinking inch by inch.

After a while of hunting offshore, it turned to face inland. Though I must have been perfectly visible, it was heading straight towards me, and straight towards the heron on the shore. I could see where this was going. About ten feet from the water's edge, the otter took a final dive, and then a few seconds later popped its head up right at the heron's feet. The heron burst into life. It took an alarmed step backwards, hooded its wings and lowered its bill menacingly. The otter turned and set off west along the waterline, rootling through the kelp leisurely but systematically. I doubt that an otter would seriously attempt to take on a heron, for they are powerful birds. It was just playing, just teasing. I imagined it having a little smirk on its face as it carried on about its business. The disgruntled heron stalked after it for a few paces, but keeping its distance. I watched the otter for the best part of a half-hour as it worked its way around the bay, keeping pace with it at a slow stroll. It seemed completely unconcerned by my presence.

I was pleased to have seen an otter, in part because seeing an otter is always going to be a good thing, and in part for reasons of vanity. I had told people back home that I was going otter-watching in the Highlands, and immediately regretted my mistake. Now, the pleasure I took would be tinged by relief at not going home empty-handed. I find it better to travel without expectation, without goals, so that I'm not setting myself up for disappointment, and can simply appreciate things for what they are.

Over the years, I have watched a lot of otters; mostly here in the Highlands, but also in Wales, and even in Asia, while taking a rowing boat out on Phewa Tal in Nepal. The lake has a backdrop of some of the highest mountains on earth; Annapurna and Dhaulagiri, and closest of all Machapuchare, the fish-tail mountain, a mountain that has never been climbed to the summit. It is a mountain of spectacular beauty, and it felt humbling and somehow comforting to be able to glance up and see a place on earth on which no foot has ever trodden. Far out across the lake I came upon a family party of six little otters, on and off the shore, in constant motion and all whickering and chittering as they went. These would have been the Asian small-clawed otter, a smaller and more sociable species than our own European otter, and the type which is most often seen in captivity. Otters talk to each other constantly, and yet I have never heard their most characteristic call, and I doubt now that I ever shall. Their contact call is a high-pitched whistle – this is often how people first become aware of the presence of otters on their local river, by hearing them whistling in the dark – but I suspect that it is too high-pitched for me; that to me it is like a dog-whistle.

The loch was Loch Sunart in the North-West Highlands, which stretches east–west between the peninsulas of Morvern and Ardnamurchan, the tip of which is the westernmost point of mainland Britain. For my first journey, I had come off-season, at the very end of November, on the cusp of the change of seasons. I had arrived through snow, the first serious fall of the year's end, and the tops were all snow-covered while here by the loch-side the oak woods were still in full leaf, in their autumn colours.

Loch Sunart is renowned for these oak woods that flank it for much of its length. This shoreside cover is perhaps one of the reasons why it is so good for otters, as well as all the streams that descend from the hills, for otters may love the sea for the bounty it brings, but they cannot survive without fresh water to wash the salt from their fur. When we think of the native woodlands of Scotland it is the Scots pine that comes first to mind, the remnants of the Caledonian forest, but these are native oak woods that have perhaps been here since the retreat of the glaciers that formed these lochs in the first place. These long lochs bring a milder, wetter, coastal climate deep into the hills. Our highest point, the summit of Ben Nevis, is only four miles from the sea; a short but steep walk will take you from a place where snow hardly ever falls up to arctic conditions where in a sheltered spot the snow may persist all summer. These western oak woods are actually a temperate rainforest. It may cause us something of a double-take, to realise that we have our own local rainforests, because we are so accustomed to thinking of rainforests as being the hot and steamy jungles of the tropics, but walking through these woods you can see it. The trunks of the trees and the boulders of the forest floor are often covered with a thick pelt of mosses, epiphytic polypody ferns hang from the boughs, and the jagged angles of the smaller branches and twigs are laced with a filigree of ash-coloured *Usnea* lichens, like a kind of alien foliage.

I first came to this area decades ago, as a twenty- or twenty-one-year-old. I had a new girlfriend, and we had uncovered a mutual ambition – to go trekking in the Andes. There was one small obstacle to our dream; our lack of resources. But this was the time of budget flights to New York, and we reckoned that once we had crossed the ocean it could cost us next to nothing. We would hitch America coast to coast, sleeping by the roadside as we went, and then we would turn our faces to the south. With a bit of luck we might even pick up some odd jobs. The idea was that we would travel without a tent or a backpack; a small shoulder bag would suffice. All we needed was a sleeping bag and a change of clothes. One change was enough, we could wash our spares when we got a chance, and could always pick up replacements; every country has clothes.

Scotland would be our dummy run. We would test our mettle, see if we had what it took to stand by the roadside all day and camp out in all weathers. We had one person to call on during our trip to Scotland, a man who lived in one of the coastal villages and ran a fishing boat out on the sound. I can't say he was then a friend – I had met him only once, when he had offered an invitation over a beer. He was the friend of a friend, the sort of person you always remember and turn to when you are travelling.

When we arrived at the village, he was getting his boat set up, so we spent the day with him out on the sound. We criss-crossed the choppy waters, hauling in the gill-nets he had laid the previous day, taking out the catch, and resetting them. He was fishing for what he called crayfish. They are more often called spiny lobsters, and though they are not closely related they do look rather like large lobsters, without the fat front claws but with long whip-like antennae, and pound for pound they are worth more than any lobster. There was a by-catch of crabs, one big salmon from a net he had laid near the mouth of a river, and a couple of real lobsters. When the day's work was done, we headed for shore with a trail of gulls in our wake. I asked our host what the crayfish tasted like. I've no idea, he said, I can't afford them. They were worth too much for him to consider eating one. They would go to smart restaurants in London, he supposed, or to the Continent, where they were considered a delicacy. The crabs he would eat. He threw them in a big chest freezer in his back room; it was already almost full to the brim. Then we went to the village pub.

At the pub, he slapped the salmon and a lobster on the bar, and the barman appraised them. These would win the three of us some bar-food and a night's free drinking. I liked this moneyless economy. Over beer, I talked with the certainty of a twenty-year-old about the principles I had been living by; that possessions are an unnecessary burden, and that it is better to own no more than can be fitted into a single small bag. Our host smiled indulgently. Surely, he said, the problem is not the things themselves but the attachment to them. Isn't it better to have anything you like, but to be able to leave it behind without a care?

I wonder. I wondered then, and in a way I'm still

wondering now, decades on, after all these years of sometimes living by these ideals, and sometimes being a little more relaxed in my approach, but still, always, to a greater or lesser degree. His point was well made, but I had my doubts as to whether, if I'd had my own well-appointed fisherman's cottage, my thirty-foot fishing boat, my freezer full of crabs, it would really have been quite so easy for me to shrug it all off without a second thought, to turn away without regret, without a backward glance.

The next morning we took to the road. We did not have an itinerary, or much of a plan beyond wanting to cover as much ground as we possibly could. Mostly we just went where the lifts led us. We crossed from Aberdeen to Oban; from the Hebrides to the Cairngorms. I remember watching puffins and grey seals off the islands. I remember a night of sleety rain when we took refuge in the waiting room of a little unmanned railway halt, and it felt like a hotel after all our nights under trees. I remember a chill night in Ullapool, where we sat on the dock and shared a bag of chips, our first hot food in days, and it felt like luxury.

I no longer have the endurance that I had back then;

I am not twenty any more. At a milder time of year I would likely still do things in much the same way, hitch-hiking and camping out, but winter was approaching and I had booked myself a week's stay at a hotel in the village of Strontian, at the head of the loch. It was way off season, such that the locals seemed a little bit bemused by my presence, here alone. It is a very beautiful part of the world but I came here for solitude, so off-season suited me better. I was the only guest at the hotel; I had paid for the cheapest room and had been upgraded to the best room, so that I woke to a panoramic view over the loch. For just two nights another guest came to stay. She was a young fish vet from Barcelona, in the area to conduct a health check on the local fish farms. I told her that I had never met a fish vet before, that I had never even known that such a job existed.

On my first morning I woke to perfect sunshine, yet with snow still on the hilltops. I was told that this was exceptional, that it could be the last sunny day of the year, and that it was not unknown for there to be rain every day for weeks on end, for though the microclimate here was strangely mild, such that the snow of the hills might not reach down to sea level for the whole winter, it nonetheless had a disproportionately high rainfall; hence the rainforest. I decided to strike out along the loch-side on the single-tracked road that led thirty miles west to Ardnamurchan Point. Almost the whole way was wooded, and I could look down through the tangle of branches to the glinting waters below, or up to the snowcap of Beinn Resipol that loomed over the valley. As I walked I was followed by little parties of long-tailed tits that looped through the trees beside me. Flocks of these little birds, with their tails longer than their bodies, are constant winter companions. They are not that closely related to the other tits, though they are often fellow travellers. They are always in groups, usually with other small birds. Today they were in the company of redpolls. They bob from tree to tree, one at a time, like a relay team, in constant fizzing motion, and in constant conversation. But this group for some reason seemed to be travelling in silence. Buzzards mewled above, and I could hear the piping of oystercatchers and the *kraak* of the ever-present herons down on the shore but not the smaller birds. About five or six miles further along the loch was a hide, nestled on a wooded promontory that looked out to Garbh Eilean, Rough Island, a small outcrop capped with trees that lies just offshore, with a fleet of rocky skerries around it that supposedly serve as a magnet to wildlife.

The hide was well appointed, and just the sort of place I would have very happily overnighted in, back in the day. It had open slots for windows that looked straight out to the islands, and no back wall, being more of a lean-to design, but it offered enough protection against the wind and rain. It has become something of the habit of a lifetime, a reflex action, to appraise the potential of every empty shack, every ruin, every bridge, as an emergency overnight shelter. I parked myself on the bench and looked out; the hide even had its own telescope. At first I could see no sign of life, but as time passed a gathering began. A seal was swimming the narrow channel between shore and island. It seemed to be enjoying itself, porpoising, leaping clear out of the water again and again, back and forth in front of me as if it was putting on a show. Eventually it hauled itself out onto the rocks at the edge of the island.

This was a harbour seal. Having spent more time out on the Hebrides than on these calm inshore waters, I was more familiar with the grey seals of wilder seas. The harbour seal is a little smaller than the grey, with a noticeably smaller head and shorter snout, and what seems like a permanent quizzical smile on its face. It is certainly more cheerful-looking than the rather doleful and lugubrious-looking grey. Neither is particularly common in global terms; the British population of both species forms a significant share of the world population. It is easy to think of the characteristic wildlife of Britain as being our land animals, our deer and fox and badger, and our songbirds, but what really marks out these small islands is our vast and convoluted coastline. The large majority of the world's gannets and shearwaters live here, for instance; birds that most of our residents may perhaps not see in a lifetime. This is our real natural glory, perched on a rock face on a wild Atlantic shore.

Soon more seals began to follow in the wake of the first. Perhaps that exuberant display, with all its noisy smack-downs onto the surface of the water, was a message from a scout, an all-clear designed to draw in the others. Before long there were six of them hauled out on the island. While greys lie flat out, with their blubber spreading around them as if they are melting in the heat, these seals have a habit of holding their heads raised up, and their tails arched upwards too, to form a seemingly uncomfortable curve, so I could not help but think that they looked like a little colony of smiles.

There was a small, dainty-looking grebe diving off to one side of the hide. A Slavonian grebe, in muted colours now for the winter. It is a bird I would love to see in its glorious summer plumage. But this would require a trip of its own; it is not a bird you are likely to stumble across, for there are perhaps only thirty pairs breeding here each summer, in a handful of Scottish lochans. Further out on the loch was what looked like a giant version of the grebe; a black-throated diver, also in its winter drabs. Closer in, floating on the channel between the island and me, was a pair of red-breasted mergansers, crisp-looking little sawbill ducks; a male and a female already paired up. We have history, this bird and me; in my years in Wales I would occasionally get to see them on the river, and finally tracked them down to their nesting site hidden in a shallow burrow on an overgrown bank – the first nesting record for the county. My long hours of closely watching this secretive bird have left me with a fondness for them, a feeling of personal attachment.

They worked the channel in perfect synchrony,

repeatedly diving for small fish. They swam side by side, almost touching, and with the female lagging behind the male by a head's length. The male would dive, and a fraction of a second later the female would follow suit. I silently counted out each dive; each one took me to a count of twenty or twenty-one, and I wondered if this consistency was down to the size of the little birds' lungs, or the depth of the waters. The male would always pop up first, with the female again a brief moment behind him. If the distance between them had widened as they broke the water's surface, they would close the gap, as if they could not bear to be parted, with an urgency that was utterly charming.

A second pair of mergansers rounded the head of the little island, also fishing, and with each dive they closed in on the first pair, as if they wanted to join them. But the first male seemed to take great exception to their presence, and especially that of a rival male. Facing the interloper, he stretched his neck upwards and tipped back his head to the sky, his sharp hooked beak opened wide. Then he lowered his head to the water, his neck stretched out ahead of him, and powered off after the intruder. The water behind him churned up in his wake as if he had a little outboard motor. The chase seemed to continue underwater, but the new pair would not be driven off; they continued to dive for fish, and seemed to make a point of rising each time as close as possible to the others, as if to deliberately annoy them. As the birds all drifted off together, still bickering, my attention was drawn to a pulse in the kelp at the water's edge right below me. It was a big male otter, almost burrowing through the fronds of seaweed that lay collapsed on the tideline. He raised his head suddenly, as if he had caught wind of me, weed draped over his head like a bonnet. Then a voice behind me said a loud hello, and he was gone in a flash.

It was a local woman who had greeted me, walking her dog. I told her she had just missed an otter, and she said she had a holt near to her home, and saw them often. She had pine martens too, living in her shed, and she put food out for them every day. They would come to her bird table daily, as regular as clockwork. Pine martens are beautiful animals, rather like giant stoats. Nationally, they are extremely rare, but here on the shores of Loch Sunart, they are more common than in other places, because of the extent of the local woodlands. They are numerous enough that they are a source of local controversy. While some locals encourage them with treats, others are trying to drive them away, for they have a reputation for raiding henhouses. I was invited to drop by and see them for myself.

It was a tempting offer, and I have no doubt that if I lived locally, I would be feeding these animals myself, and looking forward to their visits, but I could not help but think how much I would prefer to run across one unexpectedly, even if it was just a fleeting glimpse of one in the treetops, rather than seeing one by appointment. It is to do with the quality of the experience. It makes me wonder what I am actually seeing when I am out watching nature. I can see an animal in a zoo, up close and personal, and yet it feels as if it barely even counts. I can watch a television documentary, and gain an intimate insight into the private life of an animal, and yet it is no substitute at all for the real thing. Nothing can compare to the joy inspired by even a brief encounter with a scarce and beautiful wild animal in its natural element. It is not about what I have seen, it is about forging a momentary connection with the wild, and finding a place in the world for my own wild heart.

Yet if the value of such an encounter is in the raw experience of the moment, rather than the representation of it, this creates a dilemma for someone like me who wants to try to write about nature. All I can offer is a second-hand experience. I am not talking here about the sharing of information, as in a field guide or a monograph, but about observational nature writing. I can attempt to offer a snapshot of a moment in time, perhaps unrepeatable in its details, a portrait of an individual animal, at the moment that its path in life crossed with mine. I can talk about my response to this encounter, the thoughts and memories it evokes, while never forgetting that the natural world has not been placed here for my benefit; it is not here to teach us life lessons, but exists always and only for itself.

I have, in fact, seen a pine marten in the wild before, years ago when I was living in Sweden. In many respects, the landscape where I was living then was rather like a giant version of Scotland, or at least as Scotland might have been before the vast majority of the boreal forest was lost. Most of the animal life you can see in Scotland you can also see in Sweden, and in addition there was a scattering of animals that were long ago native here, but have been driven to extinction throughout the British Isles, such as elk and wolf, bear and lynx. Being surrounded by so much wildlife in Sweden had revived in me my childhood love of nature. I had thought all the knowledge I had accumulated when young had been lost in the years of city living, but in fact I had forgotten nothing. All those keenly observed childhood sightings, all the field notes taken, all the obsessive reading and studying; it was all still there, lying in abeyance, like a bird that fluttered in the back of my brain, waiting to be given its freedom and to take flight once again.

My preference since childhood had been for solitary watching, and that has remained the case ever since. But on this occasion I had a companion, a fellow enthusiast. He had returned home to Sweden after a few years away on the squatting scene in Amsterdam, bringing with him a Dutch partner and her young son, and they had settled in a little red-painted clapboard *sommarstuga* on the shores of a wooded lake. On the opposite shore was the ruin of an old limekiln, on the chimney of which was an ospreys' nest, and we often rowed out to take a closer look. Ospreys were everywhere here; they were commoner than buzzards. Every lake seemed to hold a pair, and there were lakes everywhere, but it felt like a gift to be able to watch them as they hunted and carried fish back to the nest.

On his return home, my friend had developed an overwhelming interest in nature, and birds in particular, and I was the only person he knew with whom he could share his obsession. He was a quick student; I could see that it would not be long before he knew everything that I could teach him. His English and my Swedish were at a comparable level, fluent but with gaps, so we would find ourselves from time to time in the position where we saw a bird, and were both able to recognise it, but only able to name it in our own language. So we were educating each other.

He wanted to take me to an extraordinary place he had found; a place that would require an overnight visit. We were living on the shores of the Baltic Sea, and the spot he took me to was a small, heavily wooded promontory at the water's edge. Nearly all of Sweden is thick with forest, but this was different; it was a mixed deciduous wood, mostly oak, a rare thing this far north. As midnight approached and it began to get dark, we set off. This was the northern summer, and it would be dark for only a couple of hours. We drove to the road-head, to where the wood looked black against the sky behind a latched gate. When we stepped through the gateway it was almost pitch dark beneath the trees, and the wood was roaring, so that we were almost unable to hear ourselves speak for the torrent of sound.

I have heard the nightingales sing in England. They have an astonishingly powerful voice for such a small creature, but their numbers have always been few enough that the song of each bird has been discrete; one singing in the bushes here, one in the trees across the ride, and so on. Here in the roaring wood in Sweden were so many, all invisible in the canopy of night, that it was as if the whole wood was alive with one voice. The sound poured down on us from above; it felt like nothing so much as ducking my head under a waterfall. It was almost overwhelming.

This was actually a different species from the nightingale of home. These birds were the thrush nightingale of the north, and a new encounter for me. We picked our way slowly along the path through the woods. There was barely any light under the cover of the trees, and at one point I tripped over a badger; evidently it had not been able to hear me coming. I am not sure which of us was more surprised. When we emerged from the far side of the woods it was just beginning to get light – there was the very first trace of dawn in the sky – and we sat by the shore and sipped from the flask of coffee that we had made for the trip. Beyond was a small salt-marsh, another very scarce habitat here. Most of this coast is rocky, and because the Baltic is so enclosed there is little tide and the waters are calm enough that every winter the entire sea freezes over with a thick layer of ice, thick enough that you could in theory walk over to Finland if you wished. More like a giant lake than an ocean.

A rosefinch was singing from a nearby bush, a recent arrival, a bird that had not long before irrupted from the east in one of those sudden expansions of range that some birds are prone to. A huge Caspian tern, like a tern on steroids, was patrolling the shore. A Montagu's harrier was effortlessly quartering the salt-marsh, as if gravity was a matter of no consequence. And then a pine marten padded out of the woods towards us, nose to the ground. It was a rich chestnut red, and its head was broad, so that it looked like a hybrid of weasel and otter.

At first it seemed completely oblivious to us, relaxed, inattentive. It was in its own domain; it just didn't expect to see us there, least of all in the very first light of dawn. It was close when it finally spotted us. It stood up on its back legs to get a better look at us, showing its creamy yellow underbelly. It twitched its head from side to side, giving us the once-over. It seemed more curious than nervous, but finally decided to exercise a little caution and turned to follow the woodland edge and not stray too far from cover.

This had been an incredibly rewarding short visit. Sometimes, just very occasionally, things work out like that; there is a confluence of time and place and serendipity, all conspiring together to render a perfect moment. It sometimes feels that this is what life is all about, or my life anyway; a search for the perfect moment.

I had to leave my Scottish hide in the early afternoon. At three the sun would fall behind the mountains, and by four it would be dark. This was the problem of being here at this time of year, more than the unpredictable weather, for the weather here is always going to be unpredictable. The short days would limit the amount of time I could spend out in the field, the distances I could cover.

After a mile or so I met up with a tall older man with a long staff, the first other winter walker I had come upon. We commented, of course, on how blessed we had been by the day's weather. He told me he was walking across Scotland from coast to coast. A couple more days and it would be done. He was not racing; he would walk just ten or fifteen miles a day, mostly on roads, and his wife would drive ahead in the car and wait for him. I just like to walk, he said. This seemed to me to be a very fine thing to do with your retirement. I told him about the hide and gave him directions, adding that it was a worthwhile short diversion from the road, as he would see seals, and perhaps an otter if he was lucky.

I figured that there would be enough light left for me to take the slow way back along the edge of the loch. It would mean picking my way through woods, wading through boggy ground, and bouldering my way around the rocky promontories that protruded into the loch, but would be more interesting than following the road back the way I had come.

Deep in the woods, a winter woodcock rocketed away

from my feet, like a handful of fallen autumn leaves that had suddenly burst into life. Then I came upon a grazing roe deer hind. I paused and watched her for a while; she seemed unaware of my presence and carried on feeding regardless, until after a few minutes she just melted away into cover. After the sun had dropped behind the hills of Morvern, I came upon a tall Scots pine right at the water's edge that was stuffed with herons; a roost. They looked ungainly and out of place up there, draped in the branches like badly hung laundry.

The sun had already set as I approached the village; the valley was in deep shadow and the still waters of the loch were slick and oily. The moon had risen over the loch-head, and in the far distance I could see the snow-covered caps of the Grampians, all shining like beacons. In the dark, but with a horizon all lit up by the departed sun; it brought back memories. Perhaps I have reached a point in my life where everything I see brings back memories of times long gone.

We did make it to the Andes all those years ago, my girlfriend and I. Our journey took us through a dozen countries, through border disputes, through coup attempts, but we had the invulnerability of youth on our side. We slept rough in places you really probably ought not to: Mexico City, Managua, Medellín. Our only break from the roadside came from our decision that we would agree to stay with anyone who invited us back, no matter how drunk or crazy they seemed. And so we had a few nights with a family of shellfish divers here, a night with a drug smuggler there. And finally we crossed the Andes on foot, a walk of a hundred or two hundred miles across the Cordillera Blanca of Peru, a walk that would take us over five-thousand-metre-high snow-bound passes, up among the condors, still with nothing more than a sleeping bag and a pair of trainers with string for shoelaces.

The night before we set off on this epic walk, we were on the plain, down below the foothills to the west of the range, and we took a stroll at dusk. As it grew darker night fell around us but it was still day up on the peaks and they glowed in the setting sun like a string of lights. The chain of mountains ran from as far as we could see to the north, to as far as we could see to the south, a great wall of ice that seemed to stretch away for ever. Among the mountains were Huascarán, the highest peak of the northern Andes, and the perfect ice blade of Alpamayo, often held to be one of the most beautiful mountains in the world. We walked into darkness; we would have been unable to see our way were it not for the light still being reflected off the tops. We came to a tall cactus, the height of a tree. It must have been a night-flowering cactus, for as we watched the hummingbirds began to gather around it. We could not see their colours, only their silhouettes against the snowcaps beyond. Their numbers grew as they flew in from all directions, until there were dozens of them, large and small, all buzzing around the flowers of the night.

The Land of the Lost

I woke to rain. The previous day had clearly been the exception I had been told it was; I could not expect anything other than challenging weather at this time of year. Today I would take to the woods. Though there is a bleak aesthetic beauty to the open hills, the moors and the deserts, that draws me back again and again, I am sure that if I were to live in such a place for long I would miss trees too much. Though I love the Hebrides, most of the islands have been almost entirely denuded of trees, and that was part of the attraction of coming to this area; to see the landscape more as it perhaps ought to be, in something closer to its natural state of bare mountain tops poised over wooded valleys. Though the vast majority of our forest has been lost, it still seems to be lodged in our collective unconscious. So much of our mythology, our folklore, still seems to emerge from the deep dark wood of the soul.

For those of us who are drawn to the wild, it may be

hard to acknowledge that what looks like wilderness may really be a simulacrum, just a place of temporary neglect. Almost everywhere is to some extent the product of land management. There is no terra incognita, no place where no one has staked a claim of ownership. Sometimes I wish that I could go back in time and see the world before man: pristine, untouched, before we'd had a chance to meddle with it. I imagine what it would be like to see a Scotland swathed in forest from top to bottom; the Great Wood of Caledon. There must have been that first primal observer, in whatever landscape we can visit, who in a sense first brought that place into being as a concept, as an idea. I would love to be able to view the world around me through that person's eyes, to see the world as mystery, without preconceptions. Though of course, it is quite possible that they did not see the place as beautiful, but as terrifying. I think there are two opposing desires within us; the urge to explore, to constantly break new ground, and the urge to understand, to know a place intimately and to feel rooted there, to feel a sense of belonging. I have seen this conflict playing out in my own life, that tension between the desire to constantly keep moving and the desire to feel fully at home in the place where I am.

The landscape here is actually incredibly young. The very first human visitors to these shores would have come during an interglacial period, but would have been driven away, along with everything else, as the land was scoured clean by glaciers. Ten thousand years ago, almost nothing in geological terms, this land was thick with ice, lifeless, and then as the ice slowly retreated, everything had to start again, and the forest took over the land. But the only people to have seen the Great Wood at its finest would have been the very first returnees; small bands of hunter-gatherers. It is now thought that by the time of the commencement of Neolithic farming, the forest was already in retreat due to climatic changes, was already falling back from the higher ground. Then the settlers began to clear what was left.

I walked uphill alongside the tumbling Strontian River. Up in the hills above the village are the Ariundle oak woods, a particularly fine tract of native woodland that is now a forest reserve. These woods have been here for as long as records have been kept; there is every reason to believe that the area has been continuously wooded since the retreat of the glaciers, and there can be few places where this could even be considered a possibility. In Britain forests and woods cover only about ten per cent of the land, and even this is up from the minimum, when forest cover was not much more than half that, a condition that lasted for centuries.

I worked in the forest in the years I spent in Sweden. It was perfect employment for someone with workable but rudimentary language skills. There, forest cover is over sixty per cent, the forests seem to go on for ever, and they are managed sustainably, such that as much is planted as is cut. Though I did spend a season with a team out in the deep woods, clear-felling, most of the time I was at a nursery, planting out saplings. I must have planted more than a million trees; I sometimes wonder if this will be my secret legacy, the most beneficial thing I have done with my time on earth. I wonder if it will be enough to make mine a carbon-neutral life. Yet though the endless woods of Sweden look perfectly wild and natural, they are of course all managed; felled when they reach maturity and then replanted. Just once, I visited a remote swathe of what was believed to be *urskog*, primeval forest that had never been touched. The most striking thing about it was its impenetrability; the trees were massive, huge trunks lay everywhere, trees that had silently fallen in the forest decades ago, gradually rotting into the ground in a slow, endless round of recycling. Wherever a tree had fallen was a thick tangle of young life, stretching up in a race to the sun. I imagined the place as home to wolves and bears, which it likely was. It felt mythical, almost menacing, like a forest of the imagination. It made me realise just how watered-down, just how tame, what looks like wild nature to us may actually be.

Though these hills above Strontian may have been continuously wooded for millennia, that is not to say that they have been left to their own devices. There are few really ancient trees, there has been logging for pit props for use in the mine workings in the hills above, and coppicing for charcoal for the lead-smelting works that once formed the main business of the village. It is noticeable that most of the trees seem to be of a similar size, dating from when the mines fell into disuse and coppicing largely came to an end, about a hundred and fifty years ago. And now, of course, the woods are managed as a reserve, with well-marked paths, a recommended route, signs urging me not to leave the path, little wooden bridges over the river, a boardwalk to take me through a boggy patch of alder and birch scrub, even a visitor centre.

I had the woods entirely to myself in this rain; I didn't see anyone else for the whole day. Although these woods didn't have the entirely natural appearance of a wild-wood, the trees were all native to the area, and this was ancient woodland nonetheless. If a wood is clear-felled, and then the land is worked for a while before being replanted, it will never be entirely what it once was, for a forest is not just an assemblage of trees, but a whole community of plants and animals, of mosses and ferns and moths and beetles. Many of them may never find their way back once the chain is broken.

There was a hush in the woods, nothing more than the hiss of rain on autumn leaves. In spring they would be filled with the song of migrant birds, of leaf warblers and redstarts and flycatchers. I know the life of the oak wood from my years in the hills of Wales, where the characteristic woodland was the hanging oak wood, stunted sessile oak trees that clung to the steep, rocky sides of the cwms. These too were relics; the reason they remained was because they were on land too steep to be farmed. They were often open to the sheep walk, and were heavily grazed so that little grew beneath them. They had their own beauty, for their status as relics meant that they were often in the most precarious, marginal places, and they had their own natural richness, creatures that thrived in these semi-natural conditions. There are always winners and losers; there will be some species that will benefit from an adulterated landscape more than they would have done from a landscape left in its natural state. The calls of wood warblers rang out constantly through these wide-open woods, and buzzards mewled continually overhead.

But today the woods were still. I saw no signs of bird life in this weather save for a solitary overwintering redwing. They were not lifeless, but their lushness was strictly vegetal. A thick carpet of starry mosses covered the forest floor, sweeping through like a green tide. Where there were boulders among the trees the mosses just swept over them regardless, softening their hard edges into smooth mounds. Clumps of fern emerged from every sheltered corner and hung from the crooks of the branches, and the trees were dense with lichen, so much lichen that a bare patch of bark seemed like an anomaly. I paused to examine a thick fleshy mat of *Lobaria pulmonaria*, the size of a football. Its sea-green fronds were tinged with rust red and veined with a complex pattern of ridges. Its lobes really did look lung-like, and plants are, of course, in their way, green lungs, silently inhaling and exhaling. It was a thing of beauty. It may seem perverse to have a favourite lichen, but I am something of an aficionado. As a thirteen-year-old I would go out on my walks with a pocket guide to hand that I had carefully wrapped in a dust jacket of brown parcel paper to keep it pristine. It was perhaps a conscious effort to extend my interests beyond the more obvious attractions of birds and mammals, and the orchids and butterflies that thrived on the chalk downland where I grew up. Lichens were obscure enough that almost none even had common names; it was Latin all the way, and identification could be a challenge, yet I soon found that as with most things in life, the more you know about a subject the more interesting it becomes. I had never come across this particular lichen as a child though; it was almost lost from England. It was a fine indicator of an environment in robust health as it could only thrive in the profusion that it did here where air pollution was negligible. Lichens are symbiotic organisms, not quite one thing or another; this lichen is a particular collaboration between three organisms of wildly remote descent; a fungus, an alga, and a cyanobacterium. An extraordinary piece of teamwork. It would be like me merging with a tree to make a green man.

I got out my phone to take a photo of the lichen. When I was younger I never owned a camera, part of my philosophy of having nothing. There are almost no photos of me as a young man. It was only when I had children that I used a camera, as refusing to take photos would have felt like parental neglect. But I took no pictures during all my years of early travel, as a matter of principle. I held to the view that seeing the world as a photo-opportunity would somehow contaminate the experience and stop me from really seeing. I would be considering the world in a selective way, framing it, choosing which parts to preserve and which parts to discard, recording life rather than living life. I worried that I would end up not really remembering things, but just remembering the image of things. Now, of course, I don't need to make any decision as to whether or not to have a camera; there is one fitted as standard in my mobile phone, and life has organised itself in such a way that insisting on living without one seems like such an act of stubbornness that it is beyond even me.

These woods are a key location for the highly localised chequered skipper butterfly. I will not, of course, be seeing any at this time of year, but it is nice to know that their pupae must be here somewhere in secluded tussocks at the forest's edge, waiting out the winter. The chequered skipper was originally known as an English species, native to the woods of eastern England, but they were in precipitous decline and were finally declared extinct in 1976. That would have been the end of it, but a couple of decades earlier, it was discovered that they held a remote outpost just in this particular area of Scotland, in woods close to Fort William. The two populations had been separated long enough to diverge, however, and form separate subspecies. The English variety is gone for good.

It seemed apposite to be here today; to visit a rainforest in the rain. No matter that there was not much to be seen in the way of birds and animals. To be honest, forests are seldom the best places to see wildlife, for there are too many places to hide. I recall visiting the cloud forests of

Costa Rica, a high-altitude jungle on the hills that form the volcanic spine of the isthmus. The hillsides were swathed with an unbroken dense cover of trees, through which slowly drifted thick swirls of fog. I had hoped to catch sight of the resplendent quetzal, the totemic bird of Central America, a bird with brilliant iridescent plumage and a tail twice the length of its body, but it was not to be. The rain never let up for a moment for the whole time I was there, although it never exactly fell; rather, as I was inside a rain cloud, it just hung in the air, inescapable. The one bird I did see was a solitary toucan looping from tree to tree. I walked along narrow muddy jungle trails for hours until I found an abandoned hut where I could shelter for the night, while the forest dripped all around me, and everything was sodden, including myself. I saw amphibians in plenty; garishly coloured tree frogs and luminous toads. I wish I had paid them more attention now, given them a little more appreciation. This was the last redoubt of the golden toad; less than a decade later it would be declared extinct, and I had just walked on by without paying it much mind, keen to find shelter from the rain. It was first spotted on the same exact few square kilometres of hillside in 1965, a creature that looked like a perfect effigy of a toad cast in gold, and less than twenty-five years later it was gone for ever. It has since become the poster-toad for extinction studies. Species are disappearing from the earth at a shocking rate, and amphibians are the bellwether of this great vanishing. The golden toad was hugely vulnerable to climatic change; it had a tiny range, and all it took was a brief succession of unusually dry breeding seasons for the few shallow pools in which it spawned to dry up before its eggs could hatch and its tadpoles could grow to maturity. I find it hard to bear that a unique creature, something that has been around for perhaps millions of years, should be lost on my watch, in my short lifetime, and to know that however many more billions of years the universe may last for, there will never, ever, be another golden toad.

It is the sheer finality of needless extinction that makes it so heartbreaking. With all the other threats that we have inflicted on the world, such as deforestation, air pollution, ocean acidification, overpopulation, melting ice caps, retreating glaciers, there is still some faint hope that we may be able to change our ways enough to hold back the tide, to halt the decline of the earth or even reverse it. But each extinction is a light going out that can never be switched on again, and impoverishes us all.

I walked on through the wet woods of Sunart. There is a recommended trail that follows a loop through the woods; the signs even suggest following the circuit anticlockwise rather than clockwise. I assume it is for aesthetic reasons and this route will pass through young growth, through areas of natural regeneration at the forest edge, through to the heart of the mature forest in a natural progression. I decided to break off and follow a smaller footpath that led up to the trackless moor of the hills above the woods. It is not that I wanted to avoid the crowds – there was no one else here – but where possible I like to break my own path, find my own route. I seem to have a terrible habit of losing a trail anyway. Perhaps I spend too much time watching the birds, and not enough time looking at where I am going. Perhaps there is a secret part of me that wants to be lost, that wants me to feel that I am living in a world where being utterly lost is still a possibility.

Being alone in the natural world feels like my default setting. On my own, my relationship with the world feels purer, unmediated by social considerations. I imagine that most people's biographies would contain the history of their relationship with others, and that periods of solitude would be intermissions, gaps of no account in the story of their lives. I feel my own story is that of all the times I have spent alone. Time with others is an interruption to the essence of who I am, the story of a man alone, a tale of solitude. In all the years I spent in the mountains of Wales, I had regular, if occasional, visits from friends and lovers, but these visits felt anomalous. What stands out most in my mind from all those years, is my long solitary walks in the hills, the long weeks when every night was spent sitting alone in front of a log fire, in silence, seeing no one.

Yet there have been times in my life when I surrounded myself with people. I spent many years living and working among rough sleepers, and among drug users and street drinkers, the dispossessed, and I also spent time among refugees and Gypsies; outsiders, one and all, whether by choice or by the forces of history. I like to think that I have empathy to spare, that I am open to everyone, that I will treat all people with equal respect. Empathy is not a zero sum game; caring about nature does not mean you care less about other people. It is more a matter of self-sufficiency. It is not that I do not care for other people, but rather that I do not depend on having others around me in order to feel whole.

I am sure there are many others who feel this way, people who would rather climb a mountain alone than as part of an expedition, people who feel that the many pleasures of company are optional extras, people who do not feel lonely when they are alone, people who do not think time spent in solitude is time wasted. Even during the more sociable periods of my life, it has always felt as though my natural condition, the state I know I will return to, is one in which I am out, alone, exploring the wilds and immersing myself in nature.

It has been this way for me since childhood. Not for me the football field or the youth club. I was the sort of child who, when free time allowed, was out straight after breakfast, and back when it got dark. We lived on the south coast of England. Hovering over the city of Portsmouth is a low ridge of chalk downland called Portsdown Hill, an outlier of the South Downs. From our home we could look out over the city, sandwiched between Portsmouth Harbour and Langstone Harbour, and across the Solent to the Isle of Wight. I would wander

the hill, rich with the wild flowers of the chalklands –
nitrogen-fixing plants like the trefoils and vetches – and
orchids too; vast congregations of pyramidal and spotted
orchids, and sometimes a rare gem like a bee orchid. In
my memory it is always sunny on these walks; perhaps
because they were almost a daily feature of the long
summer holidays. There were butterflies too, everywhere
the little jewels that are the common blue butterfly, and
six-spot burnet moths, with crimson patches on their
metallic greenish-black wings. I would search out their
chrysalides in the long grass, take them home and watch
while they emerged, then set them free having watched
their transformation. I would follow the fox trails through
almost impenetrably dense patches of prickly blackthorn,
tracking the foxes back to their earths. I would watch the
kestrels on their nest on a nearby chalk cliff. I would
follow the banks of chalk streams through farmers' fields
until they led me to little hidden copses.

As I grew the walks became longer and longer and I
ventured as far as the day was long. I remember one
scorching summer's day, with corn buntings singing
their scratchy song from the top of every telegraph pole
as I headed down the lanes at the back of the hill. I

wonder if the corn buntings are there still. I doubt it, for they are one of the prime examples of the calamitous decline of our farmland birds that has taken place in the course of a single human generation. In the long grasses at the foot of a field-side hedge I came upon the nest of a harvest mouse. It was the size of a tennis ball, and would probably have bounced like one, it was so tightly woven. It was presently unoccupied, for the breeding season was over, and I could not resist the temptation to disentangle it from the thin stems of grass that supported it and take it home as a precious keepsake. Its entrance hole was tiny, the size of a finger, and I felt inside. For the lining, they had selected only the finest grasses, cut into short lengths, and it was soft as cotton wool in there.

I paused at a stream through a little wood, checked a place I knew, a muddy crossing, and found the slots of roe deer, the pads of fox and badger. Far out in the lanes, the stream crossed the narrow road in a ford, and there was a little low footbridge that must have seldom seen any foot-traffic. The day was hot and still, so that the air wavered with sunlight. I paused and leaned on the rail of the bridge and watched the clear weedy water beneath. Something was nosing through the water towards me, with a mouthful of long bents of grass. It delivered them to a second water vole that sat on its haunches at the water's edge just below me, on a flat muddy beach, well trodden, behind which was their burrow. The first vole delivered its load and set off for more, while the other took the grass in its paws and dexterously chopped it up into short lengths which it carefully placed in a neat pile at its side. The animals seemed completely unconcerned by my presence and I must have watched them for an hour. It was idyllic; the lazy buzzing air of a sun-filled afternoon, the grassy scent of a summer's day, the clear water drifting beneath my feet, the quiet industry of these beautiful little animals. It felt timeless.

It was a couple of weeks before I had the chance to go back in the hope of seeing them again, and I could see before I got there that something terrible had happened. The stream-side trees had been hacked down to stumps, and the stream ground out with a bulldozer to make a muddy ditch. The voles would be gone for good. It would be decades before I saw another water vole, and that would be in a reserve, where the animals had been reintroduced and fenced in to protect them from the depredations of predatory feral mink. I was with my children, and I led them hopefully around the boardwalk through the reed beds until we finally caught a glimpse of one nose-up in the water like a miniature beaver. It meant nothing much to my kids, of course, but for me it was hugely evocative of my own lost childhood.

It must sound as though I spend my walking time dwelling on the past, but this is not the case at all. Occasionally I may see something that sparks a brief recollection, but most of the time I am looking outward, not inward, open to the world around me and its sensory experiences; this walk itself was about the colour of the autumn leaves, the scent of a fern, the texture of lichen between my fingers, the feel of the rain on my skin. It is just that when I come to reflect on the walk that I have taken then I cannot help but delve further, deeper. This is the person who is walking; I carry all these memories and experiences within me. We are all built from a shaky edifice of memories. I may choose to travel empty-handed, but I have a full stuffed backpack of life that comes with me wherever I may go. Most of the time it is buckled up tight, but as I write it is as though I have chosen to sit on some mossy stump and start to unpack, pulling things out one by one and examining them. And as I turn each thought, each memory, between my fingers, I ask myself, what is this thing? What is it doing in my baggage? Why do I carry it with me, always, rather than having just discarded it along the way?

The path led out of the woods and through a gate in a deer fence onto the open moor. The rain was getting heavier and the hilltops were completely obscured by lowering clouds. Everything was sere and russet, burnt-looking, with the rain in the air making it look as though the hillside was still smoking. Waterfalls tumbled down the hillside in narrow ravines jammed with boulders and fringed by precariously poised trees. As I climbed my route was boggy and trackless; if there had been a trail I lost it almost at once. My feet sank ankle-deep between tussocks of moor-grasses and heathers, until my walking boots became useless and I sloshed as I walked. I was soaked through; *drookit*, as the Scots would have it. They have some fine words for all manner of wet weather.

The old mine workings spread across the mountain-side in a chain, all at the same level, following the contour lines around the slopes. It was a place where two geological formations rubbed up against each other; granite to the south and gneiss to the north. In the shear zone where these two eras met, lead ores had gathered, and were first worked at the beginning of the 1700s. More recently, just thirty years ago, one of the mines was reopened and worked for barites, which had some inscrutable use in the drilling for oil at offshore oil rigs. Amongst the lead ore was found a weird profusion of crystals, not just barites, but strontianites, calcites, brewsterites, harmotomes, sphalerites, and many more. The element strontium was first identified here, isolated by Humphry Davy. There cannot be many places that have their name memorialised in the periodic table.

It had been my intention to explore the old mine workings, but time and the weather were against me, and I could see myself navigating my way around flooded potholes as darkness fell, so I decided to descend and head back through the woods. From up here I could see the full extent of the forest spread across the valley beneath me in its autumn glory, promising some little shelter from the rain that was battering against my face here on the mountain.

It had been a day's walk that was almost bereft of birds and animals. This is not particularly unusual, for even on a good day of wildlife watching there may be long waits where there is nothing much to be seen. It is what it is, and I know better than to expect otherwise. And yet the day's empty skies cannot help but remind me of a greater emptiness. With everything I see I am aware of a certain sadness as well as the joy of discovery, a kind of nostalgia. For I am watching a natural world that is already halfway lost, and is disappearing before our eyes. A veil of silence is falling over the earth.

The Singing Sands

The inevitable consequence of having a fixed base was that I could not just wander freely and stop for the night wherever I found myself. I determined that I would remedy this when the time of year allowed, but for now I would have to plan my days to include only return journeys or circular walks at best. I could at least extend my reach by hitch-hiking. Not so many people seem to hitch these days, it seems to have fallen out of favour. Perhaps these are more suspicious times, and as people have become more and more reluctant to engage with strangers, the waits for lifts have become progressively longer and longer until hitch-hiking no longer seems a viable way of getting about. But I figured it wasn't unreasonable here, where if you had no car you had no other choice, for there was only one bus a day that worked these roads.

I consider myself a good hitch-hiker in that I have what I believe to be the right attitude for it; a kind of fatalism. I am patient and I know the pitfalls, having hitched on five continents. As with watching wildlife, I travel without fixed expectations, with no deadlines. Of course it can be frustrating if I have a particularly long wait and find myself nowhere as darkness is falling. But there is absolutely nothing I can do about it; I have placed my fate in the hands of others. I have known many people who found hitching unbearably frustrating, such that it sent them into a rage. I try to avoid hitching with people who feel entitled to a lift, for it is unsettling to be trying to calmly surrender yourself to fate when you have a travelling companion who is steadily working themselves into a state of apoplexy.

For the truth is, to my eyes, that there is absolutely no reason why someone should stop for me. There could be any number of issues that lead people to pass me by; for all I know they might be about to turn off a hundred yards up the road. I do not find myself throwing curses at the receding tail lights of the cars that have not stopped, for I have expected nothing else. I am pleasantly surprised when someone actually does stop. Someone always comes in the end; of course they do. And I've met some great people hitching; a self-selecting group of the kind of people who are willing to go out of their way to help a complete stranger.

The longest wait I ever had was a little over twenty-four hours. This was in Australia, trying to get from the west to the east across the Nullarbor Plain. This dead centre of Australia is sometimes thought of as a desert, but it is more featureless than that; a seemingly endless flat plain studded with low scrub and no discernible distinguishing features. It stretches on for a thousand miles and more. I imagine if you lived here long enough the smallest variations in the topography and the quality of the scrub would begin to make it a place of beauty, a place of wonders. I was standing beside a sign that stated that it was two thousand kilometres to Adelaide. There was nowhere else I could be going really; there were no turn-offs, almost no places to stop over, just a long straight road with a service station every hundred kilometres or so, and the occasional wedge-tailed eagle scraping dead roos off the roadside. For animals that had so many hundreds of square miles to roam free in, the kangaroos seemed to have an uncanny propensity to hover at the roadside, ready to leap into the path of the occasional passing truck. You would think that the place was getting them down.

I knew it could be a long wait. I was asking someone to commit themselves to my company for the next twenty or thirty hours, and that is a big ask. But I was in no rush; my only plan was to get to South Australia in time for the start of the fruit-picking season. There was a roadhouse opposite where I could get water and sustenance if I required, and there was a little grove of gum trees where I could hide away with my sleeping bag if it turned into an overnighter.

That evening there was a sudden desert storm that seemingly came out of nowhere, a blast of icy air of tremendous power that carried driving rain. I ran at once for the shelter of the roadhouse. I say ran but I was buckled down, struggling to keep my feet. The wind tore up an isolated gum tree from its roots and sent it sailing through the air until it ripped through an overhead power line. I stopped in my tracks and watched; I had never seen anything like it in my life. By the time I reached the roadhouse and blew in through their door, they were already lighting their hurricane lamps.

I had decided now to visit the singing sands on the north coast of the Ardnamurchan peninsula. It would have been just about possible for me to walk there in a day, or to walk back, but not both. I was going there on a recommendation; people in the village had told me it was a place not to be missed. To be fair, I had only spoken to two people in the village, but both had urged me to see the place, and two out of two starts to feel like a consensus. Had it been summer this would probably have been enough to put me off, to the point where I would probably have crossed it off my mental list and headed in the opposite direction, but a beach in winter is a different proposition.

I set off from the village walking and hitching, and found a lift almost at once. My driver was only going a relatively short distance, but he too seemed keen that I should see the singing sands, and as we were chatting amiably, mostly about otters, at the point where he would have turned off he decided that he would drive me all the way there, or at least as far as the roads would take us. We drove along the shore of Loch Sunart as far as Salen, where Ardnamurchan proper begins, then north across the peninsula through Acharacle, at the edge of Loch

Shiel, and then we turned off the main road and onto narrow lanes that led across Kentra Moss. This big flat expanse is a raised blanket bog, a rare habitat indeed, bleak and otherworldly. Finally the road petered out at a locked gate behind which was a shaky-looking bridge over a wide shallow river that sprawled out as it reached the sea. This was as far as we could go by car. I asked my new friend if he would care to join me on the day's walk; in my estimation he had at least tripled the length of his journey for my benefit. But he had an appointment, so he handed me a business card and headed off, and I was on my own again.

The track led around the shore of Kentra Bay, between the birch woods and the sea. To my left was a steep jagged rock face overgrown with a tangle of slender grey trunks and a cloud of gold and red leaves the size of pennies; to my right were the flats. This was a broad shallow bay with a narrow entrance so that it was sheltered from the elements, and studded with many rocky islands streaked with dead bracken and the occasional stunted birch. Now at low tide much of the bay consisted of mudflats with a wide fringe of salt-marshes that merged into them, with curled fingers of water reaching out into the marsh. In spring these salt-marshes would be pastel pink with a carpet of sea thrift, but even now they were a beautiful luminous green quite different from the sere colours of the hills. The sky was half-and-half, quilted with little clouds, so that the sun broke through in streams, like constantly moving spotlights that gradually lit up different sections of the bay in turn with a golden glow. In the deeper channels of water that cut through the marsh were flocks of winter ducks with a scattering of waders at the water's edge, and corbies, hooded crows, stalked over the green sward in a patient search for anything edible. I paused to watch a curlew, bathing chest-deep in the water, flicking its wings and contorting itself ecstatically as it preened. Far round the edge of the bay, in the deepest channel of all, I came upon a flock of at least two hundred wigeon, and among them two pairs of goldeneye. Both of these duck species breed in tiny numbers in the Highlands, but are joined each winter by a huge influx of migrant birds from the far north.

Eventually the trail left the shoreline and rose over a hillside blanketed in a deep, dark wood. At the woodland edge was a big old house, Gothic-looking and run-down. Nothing so grand as a mansion, more an outsized farmhouse far larger than most. A row of blank windows like eyes looked out over the bay. Leading to it was an avenue of trees behind a padlocked gate. The trees had overgrown one another, tangled and meshed together to form a tunnel that looked barely head-high, and the path beneath them was thick with moss; it could surely not have seen footfall for decades. There was a sign at the gate into the woods, a warning not to leave the trail that rose through them, and not to touch anything metal in the dunes. There were unexploded munitions; the whole area had been taken over in the war as a training ground for special forces, and had never been completely cleared. I considered that you could set up a camp in these woods, and no one would ever find you; you would be almost guaranteed your privacy. I am not sure that this was the message I was meant to take home from their warning.

It was a huge plantation that stretched on for miles, and must have dated back decades, perhaps all the way back to its Ministry of Defence days. The trees to either side of the ride were great thick columns; it was like walking at the bottom of a deep trench. I thought the trees must surely be ready for logging, and wondered if the foresters would be paid danger money for their trouble. Perhaps the forest would just be written off on safety grounds, and left to its own devices. On the banks behind the ditch on either side of the track were clusters of hedgehog mushrooms, the colour of orange chalk, like chanterelles but with a dusty look about them. They don't have gills like most mushrooms, and get their name from their thousands of soft spines that look prickly but can just be brushed off. They make fine eating, with good, firm, nutty flesh, and I wondered whether, if I lived here, I would be able to resist taking my chances and scouring the woods for them. Mushrooming in a minefield.

The way through the woods continued for a couple of miles, but then the path forked and downhill to my right I could see a glimpse of sea and sand and blue islands. The plantation gave way to a fringe of birch wood, then sandy heather, then marram dunes, and finally a deep bay of white sand, secluded by granite promontories. As I had hoped at this time of year, I had the entire beach to myself; not a surfboard in sight. A few oystercatchers promenaded the shore, and a couple of mergansers were riding the waves, bobbing up and down just behind where they broke. Streams ran through the sands, meandering into tiny estuaries that took a constantly changing path across the sands to the sea. Where the waters were deep enough, they ground their own channel, flanked by crumbling miniature cliffs of sand a few inches high. In places the stream was wide enough that I had to take a run and jump across as I made my way towards the sea; in others it fanned out wide enough that I had to wade, but where it was at its widest it was also at its shallowest. In places the water had overflowed its tiny banks and had radiated thinly across the sand, leaving a tracery of black dust in convoluted streaks, like a sketch in charcoal. The patterns formed were ghostly; I could not help but see figures and images forming in the dust as I looked. This is the way the mind works; to try to form order out of chaos, to see constellations in a starry sky.

There are singing sands in scattered locations all over the world. It happens wherever conditions are just right: where the sand is the right consistency, the grains the right size, the right shape, then the sands will squeak and squeal beneath your feet as you walk over them. But today the sands were silent; they would not sing for me. I stamped and skated my way across the beach, but got only the barest response, and remained unimpressed. Perhaps, I thought, the humidity was too high and the sand was too damp to perform at its best.

A buzzard was hanging poised above the woods. There must have been a fair onshore wind, for it held its place motionless without a single wing-beat. In fact, its wings were folded close to its body so that it was not blown backwards; it was in freefall, having reduced its surface area perfectly so that it fell at just the speed that the wind blew, with constant minute adjustments that enabled it to hold its position as perfectly as a hovering kestrel. A little way along the beach there was a raven on the sand, eyeing me cautiously. I was surprised it had not flushed on my arrival. Its mate circled above us, cronking, giving its mild alarm call. I tried to reassure them by giving my rendition of their friendly contact call, but my raven is a little rusty, and I walked deeper towards the sea to circle the raven and give it space. I walked the tideline, a scatter of shells – razor shell, mussel and limpet – and the empty carapaces of shore crabs left by feeding otters.

At the edge of the bay was an outcropping of rock; pale grey granite domes twenty feet high, watermarked with barnacles. Between the rocks wound narrow ravines of sand; high-tide rivulets. I scrambled up the rocks to the summit to look down over a second bay, like a pint-sized version of the first but backed by a larger array of dunes. They were thickly overgrown with marram grass, with deep depressions between them. I found a fine hollow to give myself a moment's respite from the wind, at the foot of a tiny twisted oak like a natural bonsai; it was a good sheltered place to pause in.

Behind the dunes a little copse of trees, shaped by the wind and surrounded by a fringe of dead bracken, capped a house-sized rocky mound. It was a mix of birch and oak trees, their branches and twigs hanging low and all jagged angles from their constant battle with the wind, and thick with strands of lichen like Spanish moss. Beneath their shelter was a lawn of grass, cropped short I supposed by deer. There was a modicum of protection from the elements, yet from this elevated position still a fine view over the whole beach and over the sea to the small islands beyond. This is my spot, I thought, if I had a tent this is where I would pitch it, and if I had no tent then this is where I would lay my sleeping bag for the night. Although I had no intention of staying over at the singing sands, I could not help myself; after all the years of wild camping it was second nature to always pick the perfect spot, the place where I would choose to wake.

I made my way back along the top of the beach, where the sands met rock face and forest. High up on the beach was a long step in the sand like a frozen wave that followed the whole bay. I guessed this must be the point where the highest of high tides met the land. As I walked its length I came upon the raven once again, still grounded after all this time. It was unwilling to leave its prize, and stalked away, keeping its eye on me, before finally flushing and flying just a short safe distance. At my feet was a washed-up fishing float on which were attached perhaps a hundred fully-grown goose barnacles, with long reddish rubbery stalks like necks and beautiful smooth silvery-grey shells at their heads. The ravens had clearly been feasting here all morning; their tracks were all around like a diary of the day's events, and there was a scattering of torn-off shells littering the sand.

The barnacles did have an uncanny resemblance to the geese which I had watched flocking over the loch. Long ago it was believed that barnacle goose and goose barnacle were not just similar in appearance, but were one and the same, that the barnacle was the infant form of the bird, and that this explained the birds' sudden appearance in winter, at a time when the concept of migration was given little credence. With our greater understanding of taxonomy this may seem like nothing more than a folk tale, but we have the benefit of hindsight. The world is full of transformations – acorn to oak, egg to bird, caterpillar to butterfly. They seem just as miraculous, until you begin to learn the processes at work, and the idea that small birds might fly thousands of miles without losing their way must have seemed no less implausible. Even the great eighteenth-century naturalist Gilbert White was in two minds as to whether his swallows migrated or hibernated, and this was a man with such keen powers of observation that he was the first to distinguish the three species of leaf warbler – willow warbler, wood warbler and chiffchaff – birds that look very similar and live in similar habitats, yet have distinctive calls and habits. White's better judgement over migration was perhaps hampered by his correspondents, who were happy to regale him with anecdotes of swallows that had been dredged up by fishermen from the bottom of ponds, and subsequently revived. For it was believed that swallows not only hibernated, but hibernated underwater, a reputation perhaps inspired by the birds' habit of drinking on the wing, skimming the surface of the waters. In the end, though, White's instincts did not desert him, and he followed the evidence until he came down firmly on the side of migration.

The familiar acorn barnacle of the littoral zone, which swarms in its millions on the rocks just below the high-water mark – if it is possible to swarm while stationary – seems akin to the limpets and winkles that share its space, but barnacles are not molluscs at all. Rather they are crustaceans, more closely related to crabs than to shellfish. In their larval form they drift in the sea, and then as they mature they come ashore and cement their heads to the rocks, stratified by species. The goose barnacle does not voluntarily come ashore; it is pelagic, a wanderer of the open ocean. It will fix itself to anything that floats: driftwood, or a lost fishing float. The goose barnacle is a hitch-hiker.

Charles Darwin devoted seven years of his life to the study of barnacles, and wrote four volumes about them; two on their anatomy and taxonomy, and two on the British fossil record. These books were not among his bestsellers. Barnacles are, however, anatomically more interesting than you might imagine, as they have had to find a way to reproduce while adopting an entirely static lifestyle during adulthood. They might have adopted the more obvious method of disseminating clouds of sperm into the sea, like corals, but have instead developed a penis that is forty or fifty times their body-length, which they send out on little forays among their neighbours. Darwin's theories of species change and natural selection did not come as a sudden flash of inspiration, but were the view from the summit of a mountain of hard-won knowledge. The apparently humble barnacle forms a surprisingly significant part of Darwin's peak.

It was a walk of several miles back to the road, where I would still have to take my chances on catching a lift. Having had the beach to myself all day, I was surprised to come upon a man in the depths of the woods. He had a shotgun cocked in the crook of his arm, and was wearing a deerstalker. He asked me if I had seen a big grey fox, and happily I was unable to help him. The pine marten lady had warned me that many people locally had a relationship with wildlife that consisted almost exclusively of killing it. I recognise, of course, that if you are trying to make a living off the land then this will inevitably breed a certain lack of sentimentality, but we have to learn to progress beyond a place where we see only two types of animal: competitor or prey. It is a rather biblical outlook, to see the world solely as a resource placed there for our own benefit.

I emerged from the woods to a light shower, but I could see that the rain cloud above would quickly pass over and I would soon be back in a shaft of sunlight. The weather had held well. I paused and looked out across the bay. If summer is a wild-flower meadow on the downs, buzzing with insects, rippling with sunshine, then winter is a gust of sea air, the reek of drying seaweed, the trill of a curlew from out on the flats, frozen ice amongst the reeds, the cackle of overhead geese. This was how I passed my winter days as a child. In summer

I explored the country lanes, the chalk streams, the shrubby blackthorn copses, but in winter I headed to the sea, for this is where the birds were.

As a boy, I could see the marshes from my window on the hill; a half-hour or so would get me there. I had an annual ritual that I stuck with for years. On New Year's Day, when everybody else was sleeping off a hangover, I would rise at dawn and set off. It was almost the only time I could be guaranteed to have the place to myself, before the dog-walkers and birdwatchers arrived, before the short-eared owls had left the salt-marsh and headed back to the bare offshore islands that they called home. Flocks of many thousands of winter dunlin wheeled over the mudflats, flashing light and dark. Chevrons of little black brent geese commuted back and forth with the flow of the tides between the estuary and the grassland that abutted the marsh. I might catch a glimpse of a water rail emerging shyly from among the reeds, or a jewel of a kingfisher driven to the coast by bad weather inland. Hares ran through the frosty fields; in a month or two I might see them boxing. The place was an oasis of life. Mudflats may be inhospitable to us, but they are an incredibly productive habitat; second only to tropical rainforests, it is said, for the sheer biomass they generate. This was my winter haunt for years; I can still smell the place, the salty mud, the fermenting seaweed at the high-tide mark. But it never felt like enough for me, I always wanted more; although Farlington Marshes made a worthy nature reserve the place felt too compromised for my tastes. The sloping sea wall that bounded the place, the concrete bunkers that must have had something to do with wartime defences, the little boats anchored in the mud, the factories and warehouses across the bay, and most of all the endless background drone of traffic on the motorway; I always longed for a landscape that was truly natural, that felt unsullied.

Where I was sitting on the edge of Kentra Bay I was looking out at a big slab of rocky island directly facing me, the biggest of a scattering of islands in the shallow waters of the bay. It was rusty with bracken and heather and had a little cluster of birch trees fringing its granite face, with slender leafless branches also a fine red. I looked out across the marshland, dotted with dozens of little pools and runnels of water, and here and there a strip of bare mud, and wondered if this was a tidal island, if I might perhaps reach it dry-shod while the tide was still low.

Farlington Marshes had their own tidal island, known as Oyster Island. It was nothing like this rocky green island, just a low ridge of shingle that covered little more ground than the floor plan of a house. But it was right at the tip of the marshes where they protruded out onto the mudflats, and could be reached at low tide by a causeway of weedy, slippery rocks. There was nothing there, just a midden of oyster shells and the trace of a brick wall, perhaps the ruins of an old oyster-pickers' shelter, but if you sat on the seaward side you would be completely hidden from the view of anyone on land, and would have a closer view than anywhere else of the pintails and shelducks picking at the eelgrass, and the godwits probing in the mud. If I timed my visits just right by the tides, I would be cut off by the sea for about six hours, and would have the island entirely to myself for the whole day.

It was too late in the afternoon to take my chances on this island in Kentra Bay. Knowing my luck, I would probably end up waist-deep in mud just as it was getting dark. And I still had to make my way around the bay and across Kentra Moss before I even reached the road back to Strontian. Another day, perhaps; time and tide were not with me today.

The salt-marsh blends almost imperceptibly into the Moss, but while the marsh was still a lush green the bog was all the reds and browns of dead heath and moor-grass. It was flat and sodden, dotted with peat pools and studded with unexpected boulders, some of them truly massive; erratics dumped here by a retreating glacier long ago. It was spotting with rain and the wind was gusting, and it felt like a bleak, strange place, somewhere inimical to life. But then, right in the middle of the bog, I became aware of a faint movement, offstage left as it were, perhaps the glint of an eye peering over the heather tops at me. I paused and looked more closely, hushed and turned in a slow silent circle. I was surrounded. I had somehow walked unnoticed and unknowing into the very middle of a flock of wild geese, greylags, and now all heads were turned cautiously to me like little periscopes. Geese are notoriously shy and hard to approach, hence the wild goose chase, yet sheer obliviousness had somehow delivered me to wildfowlers' heaven. I thought that the game must be up now, and they would all take panicked flight, but no; only the very nearest stalked slowly away into cover, stately but watchful, finally taking to the air only when I began to move again, and even then only covering a short distance before settling back down just a little further off. The explanation, I think, can only be that as a single flock they saw safety in sticking together. There was no direction they could all take off to together that would not bring a share of them still closer to me than they already were.

I finally came to the road and the village of Acharacle, spread thinly along a mile of roadside on a ridge overlooking the foot of Loch Shiel. Loch Shiel stretches long and narrow from the mountains to the sea, and never quite makes it. It is a freshwater loch that drains through a short river that wraps around the northern edge of Kentra Moss. A few thousand years ago it was a sea-loch, and likely one day will return to the salt and become one again. I supposed that the ridge on which the village is set is built on moraine, pushed forward by the advancing glacier. From this elevated position I had a fine view east along the first miles of wooded loch, before it widened and kinked to the north-east for another ten miles or so. On its northern shores were the hills of Moidart, and the Rough Bounds proper.

These hills would have to wait for another time, however. This first visit was coming to an end. I turned my back to the wilds and set off along the roadside. Every time I heard a car approaching, I paused and held out my thumb. I had walked almost ten miles, and darkness had already fallen, before a car finally stopped for me.

March–April

The Crossing

Loch Morar is the deepest freshwater loch in Scotland, deeper even than Loch Ness, and like Loch Ness it has its own monster. Morag, she is called, though I was not expecting to see her. A good thing too, perhaps, for I had been told in the village that the legend was that if you saw her you would die. Though without any timescale applied this seemed a rather safe bet, for death is something of a given, monster or not. I confessed to a certain amount of healthy scepticism when it comes to cryptozoology, but my informant assured me that there were people in the village who claimed they had seen it, though he didn't tell me whether these sightings had been followed in short order by sudden unexplained deaths. He did say, though, that he thought in truth it was most likely a giant eel or something of that sort. It was a big loch, he said, and full of fish – there must be a top predator. At its deepest point the loch reaches depths of over a thousand feet, gouged out by a steep fast-flowing glacier. This is three times as deep as the North Sea; in fact, to find oceans this deep you would have to go out beyond the continental shelf, out past the Outer Hebrides, out beyond St Kilda. So who knows what monsters may dwell in its abyssal depths.

The coastal village of Morar has a single hotel and not even one shop, as I found to my cost, having planned to stock up there on supplies for my walk. It does have a railway halt, the penultimate stop on the West Highland Line, a few miles short of its terminus at the fishing port of Mallaig. Mallaig is tiny, but is bustling by comparison with Morar, for it is the ferry port for boats to the islands; to Skye, Rum, Eigg and Canna and more. There used to be a shop in Morar until about fifteen years ago, I was told by the barman of the hotel bar, but then the bypass was put in, the Road to the Isles, and that killed the village stone dead. He liked it though, he added, he liked the peace and quiet; it was like stepping back in time. See for yourself, he said. I did see for myself; I spent a couple of hours sitting in the bay window of the hotel bar, nursing a pint of bitter and a glass of malt, and in that time only one car passed. I supposed that the village just didn't have enough inhabitants to support a local shop without the addition of a little passing trade. And everybody has a car these days; everybody except me.

I had returned to the Rough Bounds once again on the cusp of the seasons. It was late March, just as winter soothes into spring. The tops were all snow-capped, more so than when I was here back in November. The spring migrants had not yet arrived, and it is not really spring until the birds come. The loch drains into the sea via the Morar, a river substantial enough for a hydroelectric dam, yet so short that you can walk its entire length in five minutes; the loch is that close to being a sea-loch. It is supposedly the shortest river in Britain and meets the sea in a shallow bay that drains as the tide turns, leaving it snaking through a vast expanse of white sands; the silver sands of Morar. The bay faces out to the Small Isles; the wild, rugged bastions of Rum, and the long plateau of Eigg, which ends in a single peak, the Sgurr, with its startling sheer cliff over a thousand feet high, that looks like a giant shark's fin on the horizon. The island of Rum was brooding, cloud-swathed on the horizon; when the clouds parted I could see its Cuillins banded with snow like a ladder into the sky. Out on the waters of the bay were wigeon, but where the river met the estuary the mergansers had gathered. They all faced upstream, swimming slowly against the flow. They were in hunting mode, their necks stretched out ahead of them with their heads just submerged. If one of them spotted a fish it would suddenly power forward, churning up the water behind it. Oystercatchers, already in pairs, were the most numerous birds here, spaced out along the water's edge, and their piping calls were a constant backdrop to the scene. Once or twice, a curlew called its plangent, rising trill. For me, this is the most evocative of all bird calls. It has a visceral effect on me, like a punch to the solar plexus. Whenever I hear it I am immediately transported back to my childhood self, wandering the marshes alone. It is as though I have been whisked back in time, and I know exactly how it feels to be young again, to feel a continuity that is somehow greater than simple memory.

This west-facing coastal stretch between Arisaig and Morar is only five or six miles by road, but perhaps twice that if you follow the ragged shoreline. It is all white sandy bays between rocky headlands. Some of the bays are huge curved expanses of pure sand rising to steep dunes, others are handkerchief-sized pockets of sand hidden among the rocks. The trees that backed the beaches were no longer the oak woods of Sunart but the red mist of the winter birch wood. What few oaks remained were small and stunted. A few miles and everything can change. There are variations in microclimate that are invisible to us. You might expect a habitat to merge and blend, to ease imperceptibly into something different, but sometimes it is not like this at all; it is more as if you have crossed an invisible line.

I set off early for the loch; the sun was shining and I knew I should take advantage of the fine weather, for it might well not last. Arriving at the foot of the loch was a spectacular sight, for the calm waters were studded with wooded islands, while in the distance behind them the head of the loch was ringed with snowy peaks that towered above them in the sunlight. Where the river met the loch was a Gothic-looking Catholic church made from deep grey stone, with a tall cylindrical tower that made it look more like it belonged somewhere in Middle Europe than here. It was named after St Cumin, a seventh-century abbot of Iona. This area has deep Catholic roots. I disturbed a pair of goldeneye, one of our rarest and most beautiful breeding ducks. They are hole-nesters, reliant on wooded loch-sides such as this. They arrive in large numbers as winter visitors but few remain to nest; the number of nesting pairs each year is in double figures only. In fact they first bred only in 1970, and have since been encouraged with nesting boxes, for in a land where most ancient trees were long ago felled, tree-holes are at a premium. I wondered if this pair would stay. I hoped so; I thought to myself that if I were a goldeneye I would make my home on one of those islands; dense with old-growth woodland, and safe from most predators. They paddled out away from the shore to safer waters, unhurried but cautiously turning to watch me again and again to make sure I wasn't pursuing them.

There was a narrow lane that followed the loch-side for the first few miles, leading to a village, or a small scattering of houses at any rate, before seemingly despairing of the terrain and becoming no more than a footpath; perhaps an old drovers' road coming down from a handful of remote crofts in the mountains, almost all abandoned long ago. In places the sheltered banks were sprinkled with the yellow of coltsfoot, celandine and primrose, the first taste of spring, and the robins were singing constantly. They are among the first of our birds to set up territories and defend them, and here they seemed to be particularly populous; they had divided up the whole length of the loch-side into short sections, so you were never out of earshot of one or more of them shouting to the world.

There are many Scottish lochs that have one or two rocky islets, capped to scenic effect with a few Scots pine trees, but this chain of islands near the head of Loch Morar is a little different. Some of the islands are much bigger, covering many acres, and every one of them is completely swathed in forest, massive full-grown pines packed densely together, so tightly spaced it looks as though, if you tried to squeeze in one single tree more, the pressure would be too much and they would all come down. From a distance they look like cushions of moss, in extraordinary contrast to the bare hills all around. They must surely have never been cleared, and look as they have always looked, a relic of primeval wilderness. It makes you pause to think; is this how the entire landscape would naturally look, would once have looked, swathed in a forest so dense you could barely slip between its trunks? In our temperate climes we are not accustomed to seeing so much life packed together in so little space; these islands look almost tropical. Although the upper slopes of these steep mountainsides are so bare with exposed grey rock that I doubt they could ever have truly supported a forest, I could nonetheless imagine this loch more like some of those I visited in Scandinavia, lakes that you suddenly come upon, hidden unexpectedly in the midst of thick woodland.

The shores and the lower hillside close to the islands were not completely treeless; there was an area of a few square miles where it looked almost as though the islands were trying to recapture the mainland. A scattering of mature Scots pines, either singly or in small copses, and denser thickets of birch or alder, interspersed with bracken and heather. This is more how we are accustomed to seeing a Scottish woodland; widely spaced, almost park-like. While the trees on the islands were arrow-straight and tall, like a plantation of firs, when it no longer has to compete for the light then the Scots pine spreads its wings, grows more like a deciduous tree, less tall but wider, more expansive, its trunk often contorted by its exposure to the winds, so it looks if anything like a giant bonsai tree. It is certainly true that in this iteration of their true selves they must be one of the most beautiful of trees, with their red, flaking, convulsed trunks, and their foliage such a deep powerful green that it is almost blue. Most of Scotland's native pine woods look like this now, wide open through overgrazing, if not by sheep then by deer, that makes regeneration an impossibility. The red deer is our largest surviving native land mammal, and would probably have been wiped out were it not for the creation of deer forests, where it was effectively protected for the hunting pleasure of the nobility. Our other native deer, the roe deer, was wiped out in England and clung on only in a few Scottish woods, but has recovered through a mixture of escapes and reintroductions, aided by a modicum of reforestation. So many of our native mammals have been lost for good, and unlike in most countries, wildlife cannot just drift back in if conditions improve.

While these relic pine woods of Scotland are not truly natural in appearance, they are nonetheless extremely pleasing to the eye. It is said that we have an innate tendency to be drawn to a landscape that is open and grassy, with scattered trees and copses and hills, and that is why we try to replicate it in our parks and gardens. It is the landscape of the East African savannah, the place where man was born, and where we did most of our growing up. Most of human history was played out there, and our spread to other climes and habitats, and different ways of living, is a very recent development. It is fundamental human nature to roam in a landscape much like this; it makes us feel at home in a way that perhaps we cannot place. These are our Elysian Fields.

I left the road, following a trail of pine trees onto a promontory that faced out onto the islands, and sat in the dappled sunlight beneath a tree right at the water's edge, looking out. I could hire a kayak, I could paddle over to the islands and explore them, pick one and camp out overnight, have it all to myself, my own little piece of wilderness. There is something very appealing about islands; their self-containment. They have indisputable limits; you can walk their bounds and feel that you know them, that you have possessed them fully. I could certainly envisage myself waking beneath the shelter of their wild forests and spending a day exploring them. But if they are truly wild, perhaps the best thing I can do is to admire them from afar, and leave them in perfect peace. It is that exploratory desire to possess the wilds for ourselves that has resulted in their disappearance. What the world needs most of all is places that no one goes; no one at all, not even me. It sometimes feels that as I advance into the wilds, the wilderness retreats from me, step by step.

Though I love my islands, and have spent much time out among the Hebrides, I have made a conscious choice on this journey to explore the peninsulas rather than the islands, at least in part for the simple reason that there is just more to see. I may not see all or even many of these lands' wild inhabitants, but at least the possibility is there. These peninsulas have many of the qualities of an island in that they are remote and not always easy to access, they are largely unpopulated and are almost surrounded by water, but that link to the mainland means that there are creatures here that once gone from the islands can never return, if they ever made it there in the first place. On the islands I may see otters and seals, and the red deer that are surprisingly good swimmers, but here on the mainland is a much wider range of surviving animals, and I could have at least a chance of roe deer as well as red, of foxes and badgers, of wildcats and pine martens, of red squirrels and arctic hares. And this island scarcity extends beyond the mammals, for many of the islands are almost bare of trees, and this habitat loss has resulted in the concomitant loss of plant and bird and insect species too. The islands do, of course, have their saving graces – the absence of predators makes them a haven for seabirds in particular – but these are islands off an island; their diversity is very limited. There are many European species that never made it across the land-bridge to Britain before the waters rose and it was islanded, and even fewer that made it further to these remoter islands. Those few that do make it may of course begin to follow their own evolutionary path – on our own islands we have the Skomer vole, the Orkney vole, the St Kilda wren – and these byways can make an island a place of extraordinary interest, but also terribly vulnerable to change.

This promontory was a rocky dome like the islands; it seemed part of the same chain, but was joined to the land by a low grassy ridge just a few feet above water level, where someone had not long ago struck camp. There was a circle of stones filled with sodden ash and surrounded by a square of fallen boughs, perhaps gathered as driftwood. There had been quite a little gathering here, and I could see why it had been chosen. It was hidden from the road though not too far away, and the view over the loch and islands to the snowcaps beyond was superb. I followed on around the edge of the steep rocky outcrop, which was like the islands but also quite unlike them. While the islands were dense with full-grown pines, here there were just a handful of relic pine trees, and the ridge was overgrown with much younger growth; birch and alder scrub with a thick understory of rhododendron. To see the forests of rhododendrons in their native Himalayas is a fine and beautiful thing, but here they are invasive. I supposed they had been introduced by the landowners at some point and had gone wild. I hoped they had not spread out to the islands. I once spent nearly a year clearing rhododendrons. They had been planted as pheasant cover, and had run riot. Every day I would head into the wood with a brush-cutter in hand, and cut my way into it. It was like holding back the tide; a few years later I returned to the place, and found it largely overrun again.

Hidden in the scrub I found a pile of rubbish from the campsite: plastic bags and food packaging, beer-cans and bottles, even, strangely, what looked like a perfectly serviceable pair of walking boots. It was frustrating; they had come to a place as pristine as this, and had not thought they should go to the trouble of taking their rubbish with them. It was too much for me to deal with single-handedly. I imagined they simply couldn't be bothered to carry it a hundred yards back to their car, and just tossed it into the undergrowth. If I was to make it over to those wild islands, perhaps this is what I would find: the remains of old campsites and a scattering of discarded litter.

At the road-head, the main trail continued close to the shore, but there was another less obvious path that cut diagonally up the steep hillside, and this was my goal; to head up to higher ground and cross the backbone of the peninsula. Almost at once I had left the scattered trees of the loch-side behind and was on open ground. The loch quickly fell from view and I was in an empty wasteland of bare rock interspersed with moor-grass and heather and the occasional boggy hollow. The sense of bleakness was exacerbated by a sudden squall that gusted with rain; the contrast with the lushness down below was dramatic, but soon the rain passed. There was little visible life; just one or two sheep. These hills must be very thinly stocked,

I thought, for there was not much here for them. Then the sun broke through the clouds, and the meadow pipits began to rise, hurling themselves into the air and then parachuting down, singing their little hearts out like low-rent skylarks. And I felt a sudden sense of loss as I realised I could not hear them at all.

The range of my hearing is very limited; I just don't have the high notes, and I lose more year on year. I remember first becoming aware of this when I was only twenty or so. I was out walking through fields with a girlfriend at dusk, I don't even remember where now, but it must have been somewhere on our travels. She was raising her voice, louder and louder, as she talked to me, and I asked her why. She said she could hardly hear herself think, for the din of the crickets. What crickets? I asked.

One by one, I am losing my birds, and I have just had to add the meadow pipit to my ever-growing list of those whose song I have lost for ever. I wonder now, if I were to return to my nightingale wood in Sweden, would I be overcome again by the torrent of song, or would there just be a big fat echoing nothing, an absence?

I don't know if it is really true that having one of your

senses diminished makes the others keener, but it certainly makes you more dependent on them, and the compensation, I think, is that it has helped make me an acute observer, and has made me appreciate what I do have. It is no great surprise that the acuity of our senses should be dulled by age. Most people will end up needing reading glasses, sooner or later, and as it is with sight so it is with hearing. But the problem I am having feels more like a sudden collapse rather than a gradual decline, and I have started from such a low baseline. When I have been to an audiology appointment, and they have tested my hearing against a series of bleeps of increasing volume and rising frequency, they have joined the dots and created a little graph, amplitude on one axis and frequency on the other. The range of my hearing in visual form looks like a low plateau – much lower than it should be – that comes to a sudden cliff edge which drops to nothing far sooner than it should. My hearing is a retreating glacier that is shrinking unconscionably fast.

It is not in my nature to be much of a planner. In deciding to visit this area of the Highlands I had no particular itinerary, I just wanted to come to a nice part of the world and roam about and take a good look at it, with no overarching route in mind. Generally I avoid preordained long-distance footpaths; I don't measure my times or my miles, and I don't make it into a competition, not even with myself. Though I like my birds, I have never felt inclined to keep a list of what I have or haven't seen. If that means that I am not a proper birder, then so be it; I am a watcher, not a collector. I have no particular desire to bag summits, though if I see a top that I like the look of then I may decide to head that way on a whim. Rather, I wake in the morning and take account of how I am feeling and what the weather is like. Then I will perhaps take a look at a map and pick an area that looks worth exploring, though even that is provisional, for if I see something that appeals as I go then I may happily deviate from my chosen course.

This is my way; I am not suggesting that it is the only way, or even the best way. There are, I suppose, as many ways to engage with the world as there are people. These are personal preferences, not rules I have made for myself. I wouldn't even claim that I deliberately avoid footpaths. They are often where they are for a reason; guided by the lay of the land, by gradients and the distribution of lakes and streams. The route I was taking was an old, long-established trail that led over the peninsula to a former settlement on its northern shores. I had been intrigued by something I had noted on the map. Up on the tops was a chain of interlinked lochans running north to south that created a long barrier, and the trail crossed them at their narrowest point. Stepping stones, the map said, and I was curious. It took me longer to get there than I had anticipated; the trail was heavy-going, steep and rocky with lots of false summits. Then the ground levelled off and I found myself crossing a boggy grassland, soft underfoot so that my boots sank almost to their tops with every step. And then I was looking down over the lochans. Lochan Stole, peaceful loch, was the largest, and was indeed broad and perfectly calm and peaceful. At the pinch point where it met Lochan Ropach there was an ancient row of boulders making the crossing, perhaps thirty feet long. It was a beautiful spot; there was something about the lightness of this touch of man on the wilderness. If it had been a more recent bridge the impact would not have been the same at all. It made me feel that we could perhaps belong in the wild places after all, without automatically destroying them for our convenience. I crossed and sat on a rock at the far side. There was a perfect silence. The blue sky and the surrounding hills were reflected in the totally calm clear waters of the two lochs. The only movement was the gentle flow of water between the rocks of the stepping stones.

Immediately after the crossing, the trail rose steeply to the final pass, cutting diagonally across the hillside. As I rose my view widened and I could see across Lochan Ropach to where a river flowed from it, and then formed a third lochan that was invisible from down below, in the lee of a great sheer crag. Something at my feet caught my notice; a gobbet of frogspawn. My first of the year, and it was far from water on a bare hillside. It must have been carried here from the waters below. At first I thought crow, but then I noticed a scat in the heather right beside the frogspawn, a small twisted scat that was greyish-white; all bone. I began to examine the footpath more carefully, looking for tracks. As a kid running wild I used to fancy myself as something of a tracker, and pored over books that showed animal tracks and trails with a dedication that schoolwork could never match. I soon picked up the trail; even here on the dry hillside there was a stickiness to the ground from that earlier shower.

I had expected fox, but these footprints were more feline than vulpine. They were fresh, recent, and led uphill ahead of me. I had heard that wildcats are less averse to water than domestic cats, and have even been known to swim on occasion, and I have heard of them taking frogs as prey, but I had not previously heard of them taking frogspawn. I imagined that I had just missed it, that it had been down at the water's edge when it saw or heard or scented my approach, and had slipped stealthily away, unnoticed.

I was able to follow its trail for a few yards only, for then it left the path and I lost it. Not such a great tracker after all. I knew there was little chance of my seeing it; it would be far away now, or perhaps watching me from somewhere on the hillside among the heather, at a safe distance. I continued my climb; I knew that I would soon reach the summit of my journey.

After the trudge of earlier in my walk, it came sooner than I expected; a sudden vista all along the sunlit length of Loch Nevis, and behind it the rugged wilds of Knoydart. The fastnesses of Knoydart are packed with the high mountains that make it almost inaccessible from the mainland – the highest, Ladhar Bheinn, is over three thousand feet high. All of them were capped with snow that merged imperceptibly into the clouds that hung over them, with none of their summits quite visible. With the mountains reflected in the waters beneath, it looked as if land and sea and sky were all merged together into one continuum. There was a sudden shadow over my head; an eagle lifting off from a ridge just fifty feet above me. It was a white-tailed eagle, a sea eagle. At such close range the size of the bird was extraordinary, for the sea eagle is even bigger than the golden eagle. It has a wingspan of eight feet, and its wings are also much deeper than those of its cousin, giving the bird its characteristic 'barn door' silhouette. It circled above me, turning its head this way and that as it scrutinised me, and slowly began to rise. Its tail was a pure, unsullied white, the white of a fresh snowfall, the white of the mountaintops around me. As it rose, circling, it began to drift back towards the lochans I had come from, and I followed below, watching as it turned in the sunshine. With each turn its tail would glint like a mirror. It circled higher and higher over Lochan Stole, becoming smaller and smaller, until I could barely see it any more, until all I could make out was that repeated glint of light, and then that too winked out as it disappeared into the clouds far above.

The sea eagle is a reintroduction, first to the island of Rum, from where it has slowly spread to the neighbouring islands and coastline, though numbers are still low enough that seeing one is something special. The sea eagle died out only in 1912, so was missing from our shores for just a generation or two. Though many of the birds I watched on my walks as a youngster are struggling, and have fallen into a precipitous decline over the course of a single human lifetime, most of the birds of prey are doing well. Through a combination of the banning of toxic pesticides and some judicious reintroductions, they have been brought back from the brink. Attitudes towards them have improved, and they face a lot less persecution than they once did, with a few exceptions, chief among them the beleaguered hen harrier, which has the misfortune of having as its primary chosen habitat the grouse moor. As a child, I watched daily the kestrels that nested just a hundred yards from my home, and once, just once, I watched in amazement as a sparrowhawk took out a starling on our garage roof. But that was it. Peregrines looked like they would go the way of the sea eagle, and the red kites that clung on in Wales were down to their last pair. Now, every city has its peregrines and sparrowhawks, and red kites soar over our motorways. My years in Wales corresponded with the extraordinary recovery of the red kite. My first two years there I saw just one a year from my window, and I would have to head far into the hills to have much chance of seeing more. Just a few years later they would be commoner than the buzzards; it would be unusual to look from my window and not have one in view somewhere in that wide vista, and every little copse held a nesting pair.

The eagle had led me back along the trail as far as the stepping stones, but I decided against retracing my steps further. There was that third lochan, a place to which no trails led, and it seemed a pity to come so close and not take the chance to explore it too. And the crags that overhung it were appealing too, a sheer buttress that faced west and then curved round to the south, no doubt overlooking Loch Morar. I figured that I could follow the waters back to the loch-side, as long as the descent was manageable. It might, of course, be the case that there was no trail for a reason, but my route began well, with level grassy ground on the shore of Lochan Ropach. The loch fed into a broad tumbling mountain stream, almost a small river, which continued a short way before filling the last in the chain of lochans. This was a little smaller than the others, but with a different ambience, for rather than being surrounded by hills, the high cliffs rose sheer above its shore. They were massive, imposing; a place that looked as if it must surely be home to eagles and peregrines. Below it was a jumble of boulders, some the size of houses and capped with heather and birch. They had fallen into piles, between which were crevices, niches, small caves, and I peered into each one, thinking, if I was a wildcat then this is where I would choose to make my home.

At the lip of the lochan, the ground suddenly fell away like at the brink of a plateau, just as the buttress of cliffs curved around to face south. There was a last massive boulder, a sentinel, just where the slopes began; if it had rolled a foot or two further it would have tumbled all the way down. The waters flowing from the lochan poured down the mountainside in a succession of waterfalls. The whole vast expanse of Loch Morar suddenly appeared in full view. I could see why there was no footpath here;

it would be too steep an ascent to make for comfortable walking, but I could see the way clear. If I took care I would have no trouble making my way back down to the shores below. I sat in the sunshine by that last fallen rock and drank in the view. It was almost sunbathing weather. I could see the whole panoply of the loch's islands spread beneath me, artfully placed like mossy boulders in a Japanese garden. And I could see beyond, to the sea, to the Sgurr of Eigg and the snowy peaks of Rum. The beauty made me want to laugh; it was almost ridiculous. I am not normally one given to talking to himself, but I unexpectedly heard myself say, I am so happy.

The Promise of Rain

While the end of March had been unseasonably warm and sunny, almost beach weather, April came bearing storm warnings. There would be at least gale force winds, all ferries had been cancelled, and the forecast was for continuous heavy rain. It would not put me off from walking. It would make for a more challenging experience, but if I had come in search of wildness, I could hardly complain if I found it.

The previous day I had taken advantage of the sunshine by following the shore. I had found long beaches of fine white quartzite sand backed by dunes and wind-carved woods, and I had found one quite different beach of shell-sand, with a dense litter of disintegrating seashells, of limpets and cockles, of mussels and winkles, of razor shells and sand gapers, and little coralline blooms that looked like tiny ossified florets of cauliflower, precious and unexpected. I could not quite work out what made this particular beach different from all the others; I could only suppose that it had a subtly different orientation against the prevailing currents, which made it the catchment area for all the less dense material from the deeps.

Between the bays were rocky headlands, sometimes backed by cliffs that I had to clamber around. This was metamorphic rock, settled in thin layers like filo pastry. Some long-ago tectonic event had contorted these layers, turning them almost ninety degrees, so that thin strips of exposed rock pointed up to the skies high above the western horizon. It was sometimes like walking on sharp knife-edges and made for heavy going. In the cliffs I found a series of hidden caves which I investigated one by one. They were small but deep, dripping with water and coated with liverworts that gradually faded away as I penetrated deeper and the light disappeared. As I emerged from one of these caves I found myself being mobbed by a rock pipit that buzzed repeatedly at my head, furious that I had invaded its home. It seemed a little early for it to be nesting, but it had apparently claimed the cave as its own. The rock pipit of these rocky shores is a bird so unobtrusive in appearance that it often escapes notice, but it is strangely confiding. Or perhaps confiding is not the right word; it is almost courageous. Walking along the jetsam of the tideline it will sometimes seem reluctant to even step out of my way; if it deigns to fly off it will as likely as not be for just a few feet. Its attitude seems to be that it belongs here, and I do not.

I sat at the tip of a headland, facing into the onshore breeze and looking out at a scatter of rocky wave-lashed islets, slick with seaweed. Currents rushed between them, and in the churning waters a diver was hunting. The bird was nearly fully dressed in its summer clothes, with bold black and white stripes on its long neck. Soon it would be gone, for this was the great northern, the largest and scarcest of our divers, and the only one which never nests here. It would be leaving imminently for the wilds of Iceland, its only nesting ground in Europe. It is really the transatlantic cousin of our own divers. The great northern diver is the loon of the Americas, the bird which Henry Thoreau chased fruitlessly around Walden Pond in a rowing boat.

In a tiny pocket-sized bay of sand hidden among the rocks I found a trail in the sand. The footprints led from the water's edge up to the top of the beach where they disappeared among the rocks. They led into what could not really be described as a cave, for at this beach everything was in miniature. It was more just a crevice between the rocks, over which a third boulder had fallen to form what looked like a scale model of a dolmen. It was a one-way trail; nothing led out, and I squatted down and peered inside. A pair of eyes glinted back at me from the deepest recesses of the hollow, and I backed away. My negligible tracking skills had led me to an otter holt. For all I knew there might be cubs inside, and the best thing I could do would be to leave them in peace.

But that was yesterday; I could not imagine that I would find any trails to follow in this wind and rain, and there would be no lounging on sunny beaches. I decided to head back to Loch Morar, and take my chances against the elements. I had been taken by the mixed woods that swept up the low hills overlooking the islands, and my map told me there were more hidden lochans up there. The first thing I saw when I set off into the rain was a bird of prey. Small and dark, it swept along in the lee of the brash of birch and bracken that backed onto the shore. It twisted and turned, following the contours of the wood just a couple of feet above the ground. It dashed, it banked and turned with perfect control even though it was flying straight into a gale force wind. My first thought was that it was a little male sparrowhawk; sparrowhawks hunt in this way, utilising cover to launch surprise attacks on their prey. But this was a falcon, a merlin down from the moors, barely larger than a blackbird. They nest high up in the hills, and in winter come down to lower ground, often to the coasts where the food is; there are slim pickings up on the moors of winter.

Loch Morar was a different beast from my visit just a couple of days before. Then it had been calm and peaceful and scenic; now, it was hard to believe that it was an inland loch rather than a sea-loch. It was dense with white-caps, and its size and great depth had delivered a rolling swell, so that waves crashed against its shore, and showered water over the loch-side road, and over me. I find a curious pleasure in being out in such wild weather; like being on a boat in rough seas, it makes me want to whoop.

The place I had chosen to depart from the loch and head inland was a moderately steep heather hillside studded with solitary Scots pines, but flanked to both sides with woods of birch and pine. A little way up the hill the slope levelled so that there was hidden ground above, out of sight of the road and of all habitation, a valley between the crags. There was something that drew me to this spot, I had noticed it on my previous visit to the loch. It felt somehow that it held promise; sometimes a particular spot can have that effect. The ground was soft underfoot and I knew my boots would not take it. I could have gone on to find a trail, but the weather was far beyond any hope of keeping dry; I might as well just accept that I was getting a soaking and live with it. I had not gone far when I came upon a fresh kill; a pair of outspread wings, and between them, just where it should be, a head, but no body at all, that had been taken. This was very recent, for blood still dripped from the stumps of the mottled wings. I picked up the skinned skull by the tip of its bill. The bill was long and straight and pale with a darker tip. It was a snipe, which has the longest bill of almost any of our birds, at least in proportion to its size, and very recently it had been living and breathing, no doubt hiding out for the day in this very spot. It had not been taken by a bird of prey, for there would have been plucked feathers scattered all around; rather this was the work of a mammal that had snipped it off at the wings and neck and carried the rest away into a hidden spot, perhaps not far away. Once again, I thought, wildcat. It felt as though I was being shadowed, that it was here somewhere, hidden among the trees, watching me cautiously as it feasted on its prize. I felt it was circling me, always just out of sight, leading me onwards into the wilds with a trail of clues, communicating with me through its absence. My spirit animal, if I was to believe in such a thing.

The taxonomy of the wildcat has proved to be a complicated business. If the population of a species becomes geographically isolated, it will gradually change over many, many generations as evolution slowly reflects the particular demands of that habitat. Eventually the animal will diverge into subspecies, and finally separate into new species. The threshold for a new species having formed is generally that enough genetic divergence has taken place for interbreeding to no longer be possible, or at least interbreeding that will produce fertile young. There are several very distinctive forms of wildcat. The European wildcat is big and bushy-tailed and tiger-striped, while the Asiatic wildcat is leaner and spotted. The African wildcats are thin-tailed and short-coated. Yet in spite of their diversity of appearance, they have not yet become separate species. They are all subspecies of the one original wildcat, in all their varied forms and habits. In fact, it seems as though every isolated population is distinct in both habits and appearance, so it was once held that there were over twenty separate subspecies. The advent of genetic testing has brought this down to a more manageable five. Of course, where you draw the line is ultimately somewhat arbitrary; change occurs as a gradient rather than as a succession of jumps.

The European wildcat was once widespread across the Continent, but its population has fragmented in response to human pressures. The changing environments and persecution that we bring have pushed the wildcat into isolated pockets of wild country. It was once thought that the long-isolated Scottish wildcat formed a subspecies of its own, though this is now held to be invalid. What is not in question is that the few remaining wildcats of Scotland are critically endangered. The domestic cat originated from the wildcat found in North Africa and the Middle East, and unlike the domestic dog, where thousands of years of selective breeding have generated a new species quite distinct from its wolf origins, the free-ranging nature of cats has left them much closer to their source material. They are a sub-species only, and this of course means that they can still interbreed with their wild relatives.

This is the real challenge for the Scottish wildcat; not habitat destruction or hunting pressure. The biggest threat to a creature that seems to almost epitomise the wilds of the Highlands is the tabby cat curled on the sofa. For wherever there are domestic cats, there are cats gone wild, strays that have turned feral; the number of wildcats that remain isolated enough to have stayed genetically uncontaminated is tiny, and the distinctive appearances and behaviours that make them what they are have been progressively watered down. It is now believed that there are more snow leopards left in the world than there are genetically pure Scottish wildcats. Does it matter that most of our surviving wildcats show some degree of hybridisation? I would think that it does, for when hybrids vastly outnumber any remaining pure wildcats then the chances of two pure-bred animals meeting become vanishingly small, and the qualities that give this iconic animal its uniqueness will gradually fade away. A last-ditch effort is being made to save the animal; wildcat havens have been set up that cover the whole of the Ardnamurchan and Morvern peninsulas. Domestic cats, feral cats, and presumably wildcat/domestic cat hybrids are being rounded up and sterilised. But what extent of hybridisation is acceptable? Five per cent of genetic material? One per cent? And who gets to decide? Conservation is a complicated business, for you cannot turn back time.

I had the pleasure of watching a wildcat in Africa. Going on safari had been an ambition of mine from early childhood. It is, of course, notoriously expensive; the hiring of four-wheel drives and possibly guides, the expensive lodges. This was not really for me, so I did what I usually do and just travelled there with no advance planning. I wild-camped without a tent, quickly learning that I would need to keep a small fire burning through the night if I was to avoid being eaten, and where travel without a vehicle was prohibited I would hang around the entrance to a game reserve with my thumb out. I found that most visitors came with a checklist of big game: lion and leopard, elephant, giraffe and zebra, hippo and rhino. But I found myself equally taken by the smaller game that people made little effort to seek out: cheetah and hunting dog, bat-eared fox and mongoose.

I had camped out for the night just outside the boundaries of the Moremi Game Reserve, at the edge of the Okavango Delta in Botswana, and I had risen at very first light. I set off walking through the long grass and scrubland and began to warm myself in the rays of the rising sun. The Kalahari nights could be cold and I had even endured frosts; another reason to keep a fire. A ratel, a honey badger, loped through the grass ahead of me. It had broad shoulders and a head like a shovel, but its movements were sinuous and graceful. And then I spotted the wildcat, sandy-coloured and long-tailed. It stalked through the grasses, then leapt and bounded as if it was playing. It seemed completely oblivious to my presence; it was perhaps unused to people and saw me as no threat. It seemed in one way out of place, such a small graceful little predator in a land of giants, but in another way it felt utterly familiar and at home; a cat just being itself in a place where it belonged. It struck me as something of a curious encounter, for there I was, on the African savannah, in the place where mankind first belonged, while the original wildcat, the ur-cat from which all other wildcats evolved, is believed to have arisen in Europe and then spread around the world from there. We were both the product of millennia-long journeys, in opposite directions.

I doubt that a wildcat here near Loch Morar would be quite so careless about being watched. I found myself in a broad valley of grass and heather moor that sloped gently down from the hills above. To either side the ridges were steeper, and craggy with bare grey rock. Down the middle of the valley floor a burn looped and wound, fringed by a lush growth of grass. There were large dense thickets of birch here and there, and small copses of Scots pine studded all around, mostly in small stands of perhaps ten or twenty trees, clustered close together to form little islands of deep green. The effect was strangely reminiscent of the savannah, in spite of the relentless rain that swept down the valley in gust after gust, like waves. The pines looked randomly placed, but I wondered whether these were really relics of a former forest, or if they had been planted like this; the effect was so decorative, so park-like, that although it looked completely natural, it was so pleasing to the eye that it was hard to credit that it had not been designed this way, that it had been created, and was a simulacrum, an improvement upon nature. I took shelter beneath the nearest stand of pines and looked over the burn and to the hills beyond. Not that there was really much in the way of shelter; the wind was so strong that it blew the rain in horizontally between the tree trunks and found ways to penetrate my rain gear. I was already soaked through, and would only get wetter, but I was enraptured. I would like to come back here with a tent, I thought; this would be the most perfect place to wake.

In this weather I had not expected to see much sign of life, but an eagle suddenly appeared, cruising low and slow down the valley, following the burn – a golden eagle, with a distinctive ragged and rain-soaked look about it. It had a missing primary feather, like a missing tooth in a comb. I would have marvelled at its size had I not seen the even larger sea eagle just a day or two before, but it was still a bird of astonishing power and grace in spite of the elements. It checked itself, drew lower, and circled, and I saw a movement beneath it. There was a small herd of six red deer hinds grazing in the long grass just over the burn. They all looked up at once. They seemed unconcerned by the eagle, but had noticed me, and were all looking intently in my direction. They were close; I could scarcely believe that I hadn't seen them until now, and they hadn't noticed me, but the rain was thick like mist, and it cast a veil, softened the edges of everything. A golden eagle circling low over a herd of red deer by a burn-side, copses of Scots pine all around, and a backdrop of heather moor leading up to pale grey crags above. It was an almost archetypical image of the Highlands, like something that belonged on the lid of a tin of shortbread.

The eagle veered away and the deer stalked sedately through the grass. There was no panic there; they were just exercising a little caution, increasing the distance between us by a few more yards. The eagle turned its attention to a ridge of the crag across the valley, and dropped low, until it was just a couple of feet above the ground. It drifted slowly along the ridge, without a single wing-beat, as if weightless, clinging to the contours of the hillside in search of small prey.

Once it was out of sight, I stepped out from among the trees and proceeded to climb the valley, following the course of the burn. The number of copses of trees gradually fell as I climbed. Eventually I reached the point where the burn met the first lochan, and the view opened out. Around the outflow, the burn was flanked by one last cluster of pines, about twenty or thirty together. Apart from at that one point, the shores of the loch were bare; I had reached the treeline. In the shelter of the trees was a pair of redwings. The redwings are our smallest thrush, with distinctive eye-stripes and a bloody gash, not on the wing, but on their flank just beneath the wing. They arrive every winter from Scandinavia in vast numbers, and then leave again in the spring. In recent years, just a very few pairs, perhaps fewer than ten, have stayed on in northern Scotland to breed. I supposed that these two birds still had time to leave, but it was nice to imagine that they might have chosen to remain, and had decided that this magical place could be a home to them. It would be a rare pleasure to hear one sing, if I still could; like most of the thrushes they have a beautiful song, which I can still recall from my years in the far north.

From beneath the trees I looked out over the lochan. Gusts of wind blew across it, stirring up the surface so that sudden shimmers of light raced across the waters towards me. There was an unexpected flash of brilliant white among the heather, and then another. A pair of wheatears – white-arses as they were originally called – bounding from rock to rock. My first of the year; in fact, my first summer migrants of the year, and here they were in the company of redwings, winter migrants. I found myself trying to recall if I had ever seen summer and winter visitors in the same place, at the same time. They must seldom meet; they come from opposite directions, at opposite ends of the year. I cannot imagine that their migration routes ever intersect. I wondered if they even noticed one another, if a bird gives any mind to another if it is not predator or prey or competitor, if it is just an irrelevance or if it is a cause of curiosity.

It was not a great surprise to see the wheatears; more of a surprise that these were the first I had seen. They are one of our very earliest migrant birds, even though they are a bird of the remote, craggy northern uplands. You might expect our first migrants to be the birds of milder southern climes, but here are the wheatears already, right on the brink of the receding snows. It must, I suppose, be something to do with the availability of their food supply; migration is always about food and survival. A few of our migrants, chiffchaffs and blackcaps among them, have begun to overwinter on the south coast as our winters have grown milder. They only leave if they have to.

It had been my intention to turn back after I had reached this point and seen the mountain lochs, but I was already soaked through – I could not really get any wetter – so I thought I might just as well surrender myself to the elements. It is often the way; if the weather is middling, you make an effort to protect yourself, seeking a little shelter from wind and rain, but there is a point of no return, where it no longer matters any more, and you just embrace the chaos. I decided to climb; I would take on the nearest low summit, where I should get a view across this whole chain of small lochs, and then I could continue, cross the peninsula and follow the shore to Mallaig.

I began to climb, sometimes following sheep trails, sometimes striking out across fields of scree, head down into the wind. Jumping a gully, I flushed a snipe from right beneath my feet. Normally they will rocket away, jinking off into the distance in a panic, but this one seemed slow and measured, perhaps needing to find its bearings against the wind. It did a fly-by, close to me, and looked calmly into my eyes. The snipe and the woodcock, with their huge black night-eyes and their steep foreheads, have a strange, inscrutable look about them, as if they are bearers of some ancient, impenetrable wisdom.

As I climbed higher, the view expanded. The little copse of pines at the first lochan looked tiny now. The middle lochan was completely bare all around, while the third and largest had a fringe of stunted birch woods around its northern shore, and an island capped with pines. I reached the low top that I had been aiming for. As I mounted the summit I stepped into the full force of the gale, and I staggered to stay on my feet. I leaned into the wind to keep my place, and the rain stung against my face like a slap. From my hilltop I could see no trace of human life, and the ferocity of the weather made this landscape seem more untamed than ever. I turned my head and sheltered my face from the elements, then struck out downhill and into the wilds.

MAY

Silent Spring

My next journey back to the Rough Bounds, as always, took me around fifteen hours on the train. It would have been quicker, and possibly cheaper, to fly partway. But I like overland travel; it gives a sense of where I am in the world, while flying feels more like teleportation. I step into a box, and when I emerge a few hours later I am somewhere utterly different, having gained nothing but a little time, and perhaps a feeling of guilt for having flown at all. No sense of progressive change in landscape and climate.

The West Highland Line is highly regarded as a train journey, and rightly so; it travels through some of Britain's wildest landscapes, and incorporates its highest railway halt, and its westernmost. From Glasgow, it first follows the shore of the Firth of Clyde, before skirting Loch Lomond and climbing into the true Highlands. For a while it follows the route of the West Highland Way, then passes through the edge of Rannoch Forest, and across the vast bleak expanses of Rannoch Moor. It wraps around the snowcaps of the Grampians to reach the coast at Fort William, at the foot of Ben Nevis, and then it crosses the foot of the Caledonian Canal. This leads down to the sea from the Great Glen, a geological rift which crosses the entire country, and marks the southern limit of the North-West Highlands, which take up around a third of the country. Then the route heads off towards the Rough Bounds and the line's terminus at the fishing port of Mallaig. The Rough Bounds proper begin at Loch Shiel, and it is true that from the moment you cross the iconic viaduct at Glenfinnan, that curves its way around the valley at the head of the loch, the landscape suddenly steps up a gear, as if crossing the threshold to another realm, the 'Highlands of the Highlands' as it is sometimes called. From here it is all densely packed rocky crags, wildwoods of oak and birch and pine, sudden lochs, and glimpses of empty bays that look out to the islands. Most noticeably of all, there are barely any houses, just a few tiny settlements and isolated halts, at least until Mallaig is reached. After wandering in the Rough Bounds, coming to Mallaig feels like visiting the fleshpots of a big city. There are fishing boats, ferries heading off to Skye and the Small Isles of Rum and Eigg, Muck and Canna. There are shops and cafés, banks and bars. There are day-trippers, come on the daily steam train that runs in the summer months. Yet the population is only in the hundreds; anywhere else it would be a small village rather than the metropolis it seems.

With a portion of the journey taking place overnight, I had arrived back in North Morar in the early afternoon, in spectacular hot sunshine. It was the latter half of May and the birches were in full leaf; the twisted oaks also had small leaves, pale and lemony green and fresh-looking. Everywhere the bracken was starting to emerge. Its fronds were as yet unfurled, still curled up into tight fists, and looked like a vast buried army punching its way out of the ground. On my two earlier visits there had been dry days and wet days, but not now. This time the Highlands were about to bake for a week in an almost unprecedented early summer hot spell, while the rain and clouds stayed elsewhere.

I set off along the shore of Loch Morar with my pack. I had no more excuse to resort to hotels; it would be all outdoors from here on. The birds were singing, and the woods were a haze of blue, for this was the peak of the bluebell season. Their scent lingered on the air, the characteristic drug-like scent of a sunny spring day in Britain. There is something soporific about that odour, in combination with the soft-edged blur of the massed ranks of hanging flowers. It is the very essence of blue, a blue that will send me into a daze, a reverie, almost taking me out of time. Britain's nature may not be especially diverse compared with many places, but it does have its highlights, and this is one of our great specialities; the bluebell is restricted to the eastern seaboard of the northern Atlantic, and the vast bulk of the world's population grows on these islands; the blue islands of spring.

Common sandpipers flushed from the shore alongside and flew in arcs away from me, keeping their distance. Their flight is utterly distinctive; they fly low to the water, their wings hooded, almost umbrella-like, so that their wingtips dip almost to the surface. And they call their piercing, insistent call, which to me has always been emblematic of summer in the uplands. But not any more. For me they are no longer sandpipers, for me they are just sand––. I can scarcely believe that I have now lost such a shrill, loud call. It starts to feel as though my world is being dismantled around me, piece by piece. It cannot help but turn my thoughts to loss in a wider sense. For every bird I hear I cannot help but think, is this the last time I will hear this song? It makes me feel a sense of nostalgia even for things that are not yet gone; it makes me pay close attention, and appreciate the full worth of everything that I still have. Perhaps it makes me value the moment more, and forces me to reflect on everything that is already lost and gone; all the things that I shall never hear, and never see. And when I see something extraordinary, an eagle or an otter, perhaps, there is a little part of me that cannot help but think, is this my last eagle? Is this my last otter? For in reality it is not the world that is leaving me, it is me that is leaving the world. It is my own absence that I am having to come to terms with. The sandpipers, I trust, will continue to call at the water's edge, just not to me, and the sun will still shine. It is reassuring to remember that the world will go on without me.

I left the loch-side and headed off into the hills. I found myself in a broad valley flanked with high rocky crags. It was a beautiful patchwork landscape. The valley was studded with rocky mounds on which grew dense copses of birch and sometimes a little oak, and there were small stands of Scots pine scattered in seemingly random clumps. On the higher, drier ground grew heather and moor-grass and emergent bracken, while on the lower, flatter ground were fields tufted with cotton-grass and little shrubs of scented bog-myrtle. The dense mats of sphagnum mosses at my feet were dotted with carnivorous plants, sundews and butterworts. As I walked across this skin of moss the ground sank and rippled beneath my feet, as if I was a pond-skater on its meniscus, walking on water. It was then that I discovered that one of my boots was leaking, badly. There was nothing I could do about it; I had no other shoes with me. For the next week I would be wet-footed whenever I was on the move, with one foot wet, one foot dry, and whenever stationary I would have one boot on and one boot off, and a sock hanging out to dry.

I began to climb up the steep flank of the valley towards the crags above, twin domes of bare rock. In a band along the valley was a dense strip of birch woodland that I would have to penetrate. On the forest floor was a jumble of moss-covered boulders that I had to scramble up on hands and feet. There was a sudden commotion as a roe deer leapt up from the hollow where it had been sleeping, and its hooves clicked against the rocks as it raced away urgently, its white rump bobbing. A willow warbler sprang from my feet and flew up to perch on the nearest branch of birch, where it looked at me accusingly. Out of long habit I had mentally marked the spot from which it had emerged, rather than letting the bird distract me, and for all its camouflage I found the nest at once, a neat dome of grasses interwoven with fresh moss, tucked into a niche between the stones, with a side entrance facing outwards. Inside were five tiny pale eggs, the promise of new life, sprinkled with reddish-brown markings. Beneath the watery light of the thick canopy of birch leaves they looked tinged with the palest blue. It was tempting to pick one out and hold its warmth in the palm of my hand, but I touched nothing, for I knew that my scent might leave a trail that predators could follow.

I emerged from the damp quietness of the wood onto the heathery hillside and climbed slowly up to the first of several small stands of Scots pine. As I reached the first I laid my hand against its trunk as if touching a talisman, and turned to look back. I had climbed a few hundred feet and the landscape had opened out. I could see over the tops to a chain of small lochans that in this sunshine were an astonishing ultramarine blue, a far deeper blue than the sky, and on the horizon I could see the jagged peaks of the Cuillins of Skye, still streaked in places with the last of the snow.

I took a break beneath the pines to cool down from the climb; one boot off, of course. I feel at home among the pines; we have so much history. The Scots pine has a huge range, for all that it has a name in English that makes it sound like a local speciality. It grows all across northern Europe, and in mountains further south, it blankets Scandinavia up to above the Arctic Circle, and it reaches all across Russia as far as eastern Siberia, forming a significant part of the taiga, the largest expanse of woodland in the world, larger even than the Amazon rainforest. This was the tree that I planted out in my years in Sweden, where a million of their saplings passed through my hands. And when I finished work, these were the woods I walked through. When I looked out over the Baltic Sea from my home on the coast, there were thousands of tiny rocky islands, almost all unin-habited, which I could row out to, and each one was capped with a little fringe of Scots pines. When I lived in

Wales, too, my cottage was high on a hillside beneath a plantation of them. As the years passed, I watched this wood grow from a dense, impenetrable thicket to a fine stand of mature trees, helped by me along the way, for I spent a year in there with my chainsaw, thinning it out to give it space to breathe.

These relic woods in Scotland are thought to cover just one per cent of their original range. They cannot regenerate naturally; if mankind were suddenly to vanish completely from the Highlands they would still not grow back. There are simply too many deer, and since we killed the last of the wolves a few hundred years ago the red deer has no natural predators. Change one thing and you change everything, in a cascade of cause and effect. Attempts are being made in places to replant these native woods in areas of moorland protected by deer fences. A replanted wood will never be a wildwood, it will always be a simulacrum, yet it is being handled with care and thoughtfulness. Rather than just replanting bare patches of moorland, the existing fragments of pine wood are being allowed to expand into the hills around them. Eventually, perhaps, these last relics of the once great wood could begin to join together. It will not happen in my lifetime, but perhaps one day the forest will be reborn. The red deer will not mind; the irony is that they are by nature creatures of the forest, and have had to adapt to living on open ground.

I finally reached the summit of the ridge and threw down my pack. The day was hot and I was overdressed. There was a steep drop beneath me, down to a small loch studded with islands, and the steepness of this hillside had perhaps protected it, for it was covered with a dense stand of pines. The loch looked incredibly inviting, and after a pause for breath I began to slither down the slopes, heading from tree trunk to tree trunk to slow my descent. At one point I came to a sheer drop, perhaps fifty feet of cliff, and I picked my way down carefully, handhold by handhold on the bare rock. Further down, the ground levelled off a little, and the pine wood had an understorey of young birch, and beneath that a ground layer that was carpeted with bluebells and primroses and violets. It was idyllic.

Mostly the hillside fell straight into the waters of the loch, but there was a little bay in the lee of the nearest islands, and a tiny blanket-sized strip of sand, so that would be my beach. I am not a dedicated wild swimmer, in that I do not set out to a destination with the specific intent of taking a swim. I am more of an opportunist; if the right circumstances arise then I will take advantage of them. And this was the perfect opportunity; I was overheated from a stiff uphill walk, the sun was shining and I was in a perfect spot that I had all to myself. There was a little pine-topped island just fifty yards out that made a tempting destination. So I stripped off and waded into the shallows. The water was silky and not as cold as I had expected; I supposed that this loch was not so deep, and I was sure that the thousand-foot-deep Loch Morar would still be icy. I breast-stroked my way across to the little island and clambered up its rocky sides. An island of my own; it did cross my mind that I could pitch my tent here and make this my camp. The water was fairly shallow close to the shore, and I could probably just about have waded out to the island with my pack held above my head. But the island was rocky and beneath the pines was an undergrowth of three-foot-high scratchy heather. So instead I continued my swim, doing a little circuit of the bay.

I am not a strong swimmer, and avoided going too far out. As a child I was never allowed to swim, because of the chronic ear infections that had plagued my early years and left my hearing so impaired. I did not finally teach myself to swim until I was twenty or so. I was trekking in the jungles of southern Mexico, close to the Mayan ruins of Palenque. It was so hot and humid that I was breaking out in prickly heat; dozens of tiny sweat bubbles beneath my skin, the first and only time I have ever suffered from this. I came to a stream through the jungle, which fell down a hillside in a series of waterfalls, beneath each of which was a swimming-hole of crystal-clear water, and without really thinking I jumped in and found that I could indeed swim, I just didn't know it. From that point on, I swam at every opportunity, without ever becoming particularly proficient.

A few years later, snorkelling off an island on the Great Barrier Reef, I became distracted by the incredible spectacle, the sheer profusion of corals and tropical fish, and noticed too late that the shore had become much further away than I had anticipated. And no matter how hard I swam back towards the shore, it became still further away; I had been caught by an undertow and was being steadily sucked out to sea. By the time the lifeguards reached me I was spending more time beneath the surface than above it. I had not realised that my predicament had been spotted, and had accepted that this was likely the end of my story. My life did not flash before my eyes; rather, I felt annoyance at the carelessness that had led me to such a foolish way to die, and I felt sorrow too, for there were so many things that I still wanted to see, wanted to do. That night, back on the mainland, I was unable to sleep, for I had broken out in a sudden high fever. I walked along the edge of a forest of gum trees, clouds of fruit bats passing in a great stream through the canopy. Each time I inhaled, it was like a knife to the chest. The water in my lungs had turned to pneumonia. I would spend several days in hospital in Cairns, on an oxygen inhaler and with an antibiotic drip. They told me I was lucky that it was seawater I had inhaled, rather than fresh water, for reasons to do with osmosis, I suppose. Luck is relative, and ever since then I have taken more responsibility for my own luck when it came to water, and treated it with greater respect.

As I swam, a pair of water birds emerged from the dense vegetation at the water's edge, and began to sail towards me. I supposed that perhaps my crashing down the hillside had caused them to hide beneath the bank, but now that I was silently immersed in water and only a head high, I seemed more harmless. In fact, they seemed to regard me now more as an object of curiosity than as a possible threat, for they swam closer and closer. I stopped my swimming and held still, expecting at any moment for them to back away, watching at eye level as they approached. Their bodies were a deep coppery red, their wings black, their heads crested and their eyes a startling crimson. They were Slavonian grebes, a bird that really should not have been here. This is the bird that I had watched on Loch Sunart in the winter, a bird that I regretted I would not see in its glorious summer plumage. The few pairs that stay on when winter ends are restricted to a very small area of the Eastern Highlands, far from here. As I cooled off in the little hidden bay, with primeval forest all around, the sun beating down from above, and these extraordinary, implausible creatures drifted ever closer, I felt disconnected from the world, out of place and out of time. I felt I had been transported for a moment to an alternate reality; a better reality. These birds are very late nesters, and the truth, I supposed, was that they were yet to head to their nesting grounds in the east, but seeing them here now was not something that I could ever have anticipated.

The birds turned suddenly, and swam quickly back to shore. I had made no unexpected movements; this was not about me. I lay on my back in the water and looked up. High above, a golden eagle was circling the grey crags from where I had descended. After a moment it was joined by a second bird, and the two of them circled lazily overhead, watching me, I think, trying to make sense of what I was, and what I was doing there.

I spent the day aimlessly wandering the hills, with no destination save for the expectation of seeking out a suitable location to camp for a day or two. Meadow pipits sprang from my feet, then fell to the ground a few feet away, broken-winged. Rather than searching out their nests I humoured them, following them for a few feet until they would suddenly recover their strength and take to the air, victorious. I liked to imagine them congratulating themselves over how clever their deception had been. They were everywhere in these hills, singing and calling, though of course to me they were no longer pipits, they were just —its.

These moors and bogs were trackless, save for the

occasional sheep or deer trail. The stocking levels on these hills were so low that I might have walked for an hour or two without seeing a single sheep, but they still left their mark. I find it hard to resist falling in with a track when I come across one, and they occasionally serve to lead me around a rocky outcrop or across boggy ground with a degree of efficiency, but for the most part they are a false promise. They may look as though they are going somewhere, but the priorities of sheep are different from ours, and they are likely to lead only to where the grass is greenest.

There is one more quality to these hills which adds to their sense of isolation, beyond their physical inaccessibility, and that is that they almost entirely lack a mobile phone signal. I would not be receiving any sudden phone calls or texts, would not be tempted to check my emails or try to contact anyone even if I wanted to. If I got into difficulties it would be entirely up to me to get myself out of them. Even when we are alone it is only a provisional solitude if the world is only a click away. Travel nowadays is a very different experience. When I first travelled people would expect me to be entirely out of reach for, say, six months; they might perhaps receive a postcard telling them where I had been a couple of weeks ago, but had no way of responding. Now, there is an internet café on every corner, people can update their travel blogs daily, there is GPS tracking and live video chat. What is meant now by being alone is not what it used to mean. It is, of course, possible to opt out of all this, but it demands a mental shift; we have come very quickly to accept it as the norm that we are contactable at all times.

I found my spot, beneath a wizened oak tree at the edge of a fine birch wood that clung to a ridge in a craggy valley, and overlooked a winding burn. Not far upstream, this burn ran fast and narrow down a series of waterfalls, but here the valley floor levelled and the stream widened and deepened and coiled between boggy water meadows, flat and lush, that extended about a hundred yards to each side of the winding stream. I faced out to a fine stand of pines and above to bare grey cliffs in which were a couple of small caves. I pitched my tent, a tiny one-man mountain tent good only for sleeping, not for sitting up in. The oak had a thick root-bole, and the trunk leaned back, providing me with a perfect seat where I could kick back and while away my time looking out over the stream and up and down the valley. The tent was unavoidable, I had decided, not so much because of the unpredictability of the weather as because of the fact that midge season had begun.

If my first trip had been all about the otters, and my second about the eagles, I was seriously hoping that the key species of this visit would not turn out to be *Culicoides impunctatus*. The Highland midge can descend in vast clouds, drawn in by the gradient of carbon dioxide from your breath. They don't really hurt – much more problematic are the ticks that can carry Lyme disease, and one of which I had already removed from my groin – but even for someone as phlegmatic as myself, they can be utterly infuriating. I tell myself how lucky it is that only the females draw blood, as part of my lifelong quest to look for the bright side in anything, but it doesn't help all that much; the difference between a cloud of a million and a cloud of two million is ultimately an academic one. Arguably, though, they are guardians of the wilderness; there can be no doubt that they help keep visitor numbers down, and help keep the place wild and unpopulated. It sometimes seems as though all the most attractive destinations have their own special curse; the snake in the garden. I recall the coral cayes of Belize, which had some of the most beautiful deserted beaches I have ever seen. Deserted for a reason; you could barely walk on them, and certainly not stand still on them for even the briefest moment, because of the sand fleas, almost invisibly small biting midges that would attack like a thousand miniature hypodermic syringes, starting at your ankles and working very quickly up. Camping out on one of these islands, with no tent, I couldn't sleep on the beaches because of the sand fleas, and I couldn't sleep inland because of the vast hordes of land crabs that came out to prowl every night, and were so numerous that you couldn't walk after dark without hearing the crunch of them beneath your feet. I resorted to a long-abandoned wooden hut on an uninhabited beach, raised on stilts, but even then as dawn approached it was invaded, and I moved to an old wooden jetty, and slept out at its tip, over water.

This evening, at least, the midges were not being too unmanageable. There was a pleasant breeze blowing, which kept them at bay. Whenever the breeze dropped, they would suddenly appear as if from nowhere, but the wind would soon pick up again and drive them away. Having pitched my tent, I decided I would use this as my base for a couple of days. I am not about the distance covered; I would win no prizes for my abilities as a long-distance walker. I don't count my miles, or set myself goals; peaks to conquer, targets to be met. I know that many people like to engage with the natural world as a sport, a personal challenge, but I am more interested in quality, the depth of experience rather than the quantity of it. I would probably count a day in which I had not gone far as more of a success than a day when I had gone twice the distance, for it would indicate that there had been more worthwhile distractions along the way. When I was younger, I was perhaps more greedy in my ambitions; I wanted to see everything and go everywhere. But I came to realise that trying to quantify experience is meaningless. Spending a month in one country could offer just as much diversity of experience as spending a fortnight each in two countries, and so I made a conscious decision after I had passed the fifty-country mark to simply stop counting. And this felt liberating, in that if I liked a place I would stay as long as I wanted rather than chasing borders, rather than every arrival being filled with thoughts of departure. I imagine that a fit and determined hiker could complete a circuit of the Rough

Bounds in about a week. For me, with all my diversions and digressions, my retracing of steps already taken and my self-imposed delays, I envisaged that my own circuit would probably take up more than a month of walking. And I would still feel that I had barely skimmed the surface.

The burn in the water meadows ahead of me seemed unfordable, deep and muddy and fringed with sedges, but a little way downstream in the woods the stream broadened to white water over shingle, so I took off my boots, rolled up my jeans, and waded across. Grey wagtails bobbed from stone to stone, and a little troop of tiny ducklings scooted away to hide under the banks. I walked through the pines and began to ascend. My goal was to investigate the caves on the hillside opposite. There is something alluring about caves; it seems impossible to pass one by without pausing to investigate. Perhaps it is an ancestral thing; a collective memory of a primeval past. I could also not help but check every plausible niche in the vain hope of running into a wildcat. As I climbed the slope towards the caves, I came upon a small herd of grazing roe deer. They jumped as they saw me, and clattered off over the rocky ridge like chamois in the Alps. When I reached the place they had been grazing, I stumbled upon the skeleton of a roe buck, long stripped clean of any trace of flesh or fur. The skull was detached from the body, and a little distance away, and I picked it up and looked it over. It was a strangely beautiful thing; the long graceful lines of its slender snout, the seemingly placid gaze of its empty orbits. It had one fine antler, but the other was snapped off halfway down. I wondered if this had happened at the time it had died; in the rutting season roebucks will sometimes fight to the death.

When I visited in the winter, I had the problem of having to abort my walks in early afternoon, because it was dark by four. Now I had the opposite problem; there were nearly eighteen hours of light, and I cannot walk for eighteen hours. I would spend the evening sitting at my campsite, watching the swallows swooping over the water meadows, and the occasional heron or flight of mallards parading up and down the valley, following the turns of the burn, and hoping that the breeze would hold. I had decided to opt for the lowest-impact camping possible. I would light no fires, and had not even brought a camping stove with me, as part of my quest to travel as light as possible. I figured that I could manage without hot food for a couple of days; the hardest thing would be going without my morning coffee.

At first I felt strangely restless and unsettled; I kept getting up and pacing a little way along the stream or into the woods. I had been on the move all day, and sometimes it is easier to keep moving than it is to stay still. I knew that this would pass, though; it just takes a little time. I needed to settle into the spirit of the place. The art of staying still, and paying close attention, is one worth cultivating. As the day drifted into the gloaming, the long drawn-out half-light of the northern summer, I began to ease my way into stillness, a slower way of thinking and moving, but with a greater alertness. I spent so much time in my years in Wales sitting quiet and still, that it feels as though this is my essential way of being, that the rest is just distraction. This is what can happen when you are completely alone in nature; you may see the same things as when you are in company, but you see them quite differently. You slough off the skin of self, all self-awareness, and are left with pure sensation. Nothing has a name; it is only itself. You look at a tree, and instead of seeing it as an idea, a network of associations built up over a lifetime, you see it for itself, pure form, freed of all preconceptions. You see the play of light, and everything is radiant, everything is in fact made of light. I have had moments like this since childhood, moments when I felt that I had stepped out of time, moments when I felt as though there was no longer any filter between me and the world; the filter being, I suppose, the carefully constructed self.

As the light began to fade, deer emerged from the woods. First, a group of three began to graze well upstream from me, up by the waterfalls. Then a single buck came out of the pine woods opposite to drink from the stream. It must have scented me, or seen me, or heard me, for it suddenly jumped backwards and fled back into the woods. As it did so, it barked four times in quick succession. To dub this alarm call a bark is not to do it justice: it was fierce and explosive and it echoed against the crags so that it filled the whole valley. In spite of that, a little herd of five yearlings soon followed, delicately crossing the stream at the ford that I had earlier used myself. They began to graze on the water meadow between me and the stream, coming ever closer, and as slowly and quietly as I could I slipped inside my tent so they would not see me, and watched from within. This valley really was roe deer heaven. They came ever closer, until they were all around my tent, just feet away, so close that I would eventually fall asleep to the sound of munching grass.

I woke at first light to the insistent call of a cuckoo. Realising I would not get back to sleep, I rose and strolled into the wood. The sunlight streamed in slantwise, almost horizontally, lighting up the forest floor more brightly than it ever would when the sun was high, all endless shadows and glints of light between the birch trunks. The dawn chorus had started up; I could hear the thrushes and the finches singing. These northern birch woods don't support the same diversity and density of birds as, say, a southern oak wood, and so it could hardly compare to those dawn choruses long ago. I told myself this, but it was pointless; who did I think I was trying to fool? I could see the warblers in the trees, their beaks agape. But the songs of these wood warblers and willow warblers were now also lost to me; what remained were just woods and willows, followed by an absence, a void.

My time was coming, my own personal silent spring. It would, of course, be possible for me to pass through life not hearing certain sounds without ever realising that I was missing out. The world is filled with things that are beyond our perception, of which we are never made aware. This silence had no doubt been creeping up on me for years in the city without my ever being fully conscious of it. It takes a very specific set of circumstances for it to come to my notice; it takes the focused attention that I devote to the world when I am out in nature for me to see where there would once have been a sound, where there should be a sound, only to find that it has abandoned me.

On a muddy deer path within the wood, I found a single perfect fresh pad-mark, crossing the path rather than following it, facing towards my tent. A wildcat had come to visit me in the night, silent and unseen in the darkness. Of course it had. The world is full of hidden things.

The Point and the Sound

The Rhu of Arisaig is a small, almost uninhabited west coast peninsula. To its north is a little sheltered bay, Loch nan Ceall, at the head of which is the village of Arisaig. In this harbour are moored perhaps twenty or thirty sailing boats, and people learn to kayak in its calm, shallow waters. A road extends from the village partway along the northern shore of the peninsula, and along this are scattered a bare handful of houses, but the southern shores of the Rhu, facing out to the much larger and wilder Sound of Arisaig, are completely depopulated.

I say depopulated, rather than uninhabited, advisedly. It is easy to look at a wild landscape and to assume that it was ever thus, that there is a steady progression over time from wilderness to civilisation, but this is not always the case, especially so in the Western Highlands. There was a time when many more people lived off this land than now. Two hundred years ago, there were perhaps fifty crofts on the Rhu, but when sheep-farming became the vogue among Scottish landowners, the land's prior occupants were considered dispensable, and the clearances began. Many emigrated to the Americas, while those who remained were relocated in towns and villages away from the area. The whole of this peninsula became a single sheep farm.

While the Rough Bounds were always isolated from most of the mainland, the fact that there were virtually no roads did not mean there was no communication, for there were still sea-roads. Getting from place to place was almost always easier by water, and the area's links were more with the islands than the interior. There was a thriving community here once. It can be seen in the place names, the fact that almost every little hill and tiny lochan has a name, showing it was once of significance to someone.

And occupation of this land dates back further, much further. I was on a hillside on the south side of the peninsula, far from the nearest road or house, looking down at a Neolithic relic, which showed that while it might be uninhabited now, there were people here five thousand years ago. I had spotted it on my map – 'cup-marked stone', written in a Gothic script, and then I had read a little about it in the visitor centre in the village. It had been my intention to cross the peninsula and then head back along the coastline over the course of a couple of days, so it was just a matter of plotting the right line over the hills, in order not to miss it. The stone was sited on a steep grassy hillside facing south. There was a single tree nearby, and a single grazing sheep, watching me cautiously. A big smoothed slab of rock bulged from the long grass. Its entire surface was covered with dozens of small shallow discs that had been scraped into it, all different sizes, and in its centre a single large deep cup filled with rainwater.

There were legends associated with this cup-stone. The blacksmith's son would be brought here to wash his hands in the cup of rain; it would give him strength and skill. Earlier than that, the legend had it that if you circuited the stone three times while chanting in Gaelic, it would offer protection against witchcraft. This stone long predated blacksmiths, or Gaelic, of course. Cup-marked stones are found scattered throughout Europe, and we can only speculate as to their significance. They are not quite a *tabula rasa*, a blank slate, but they are abstract enough that they invite us to project our own desires, our own meanings onto them. As I looked over the face of the stone, what I saw was a pattern of stars, with a great sun at its centre. I imagined it once having been aligned with the setting sun, or the rising sun, and this site having its own ritual significance in its creators' understanding of cosmology and the turn of the seasons.

We tend to think of sun worship as the most primitive of religions, but it seems to me that it has a kind of logic based on the visible – far more so than the religions that came later, where man began to create gods in his own image. The sun, after all, is the source of all life, and each night it departs, leaving us hoping that it will return at its appointed time. The sun is demonstrably central to life on earth, and man is not, yet we have convinced ourselves that the world is actually all about us. So I look at the stone and see my own prejudices reflected back at me. It is all speculative; for all I know the cup might have been used as the repository for the blood of human sacrifices. All it can really tell me is that there were people here on these shores long ago, when the land was still unworked and pristine; people in search of meaning. I plunged my hands into the deep cup of rainwater, and rinsed them, out of respect. It was a perfect fit for my two hands together.

Little is known of the ancient inhabitants of these lands. In around the year 150 AD, Ptolemy wrote his *Geography*, and in his account of the tribes of Albion he identified one known as the Creones, whose home range corresponded almost exactly with the limits of the Rough Bounds. There is absolutely no written record of these people, not even of their existence, beyond that one single mention by Ptolemy.

Sometimes I feel it is good to know and to have certainty, but sometimes also a little ambiguity is a powerful thing and can inspire the imagination. Here, there are not many birds or animals or plants that can get past me without my being able to identify them, name them, or have some idea of their place in the scheme of things. But it can be worthwhile to get out of my comfort zone, too. If I travel to the tropics, or the South, I can find myself unmoored. In the hills of Rwanda, I watched a mixed flock of birds descending on a flowering shrub, and was completely unable to identify a single one, or even the family to which it belonged; nor was I able to identify the plant on which it was feeding. It is useful to be reminded of your place, and to recognise just how much you still have to learn, and how much you will never know.

From the hillside of the cup-stone it was downhill all the way to the southern shore, a curved bay of grey pebbles, low cliffs with the promise of caves and a straggle of birch wood at their foot. These cliffs were set back a little from the shore; they had once been sea cliffs, and the caves that studded them had been sea caves, before the land had rebounded after the melting of the glaciers that had crushed the land down with the weight of all that ice. Beneath them was a rocky sea-splashed platform and a jumble of fallen boulders; I knew that much of the time I would be bouldering and scrambling rock to rock, rather than walking. Sometimes above the splash zone there would be a strip of grass where walking was possible, and misshapen birch trees clung to the lower slopes. Out towards the end of the headland something ran from my feet – a sandpiper. I looked down and sheltered beneath a frond of dead bracken was a little grassy cup, and in it four mottled eggs. They were neatly placed, with their four thick ends touching in the very centre of the nest, so that they looked like the four points of a compass.

When I reached the final point of the headland I could see ahead, all the way along the coast to my chosen camping spot. Most of the bays along this shore were rocky, but I had found a single sandy beach on my map a few miles along the coast and had decided to make that my destination. I could see that it would take me hours; it would be very slow-going indeed, for this shoreline was ragged and broken. There would be no path, it would be rock to barnacled rock, traverses of low cliffs, the occasional hopeful leap. Sometimes I would be forced below the high-water mark, and would find myself slipping and sliding over dense mats of bladderwrack that hid the rocks beneath, while oystercatchers followed my slow progress, calling in frustration at my invasion of their territory.

I would have to earn this walk. It would be like climbing a mountain packed with false summits. I would round a headland expecting to see a spread of sand, and would find yet another bay of stones. At one, I saw that I had company; a sea kayaker pulling up his boat onto the beach. When I come across someone else out in the wilds, I try to pick a line that will mean our paths do not intersect. I work on the assumption that they, like me, would prefer to remain alone, and they are not seeking out conversation. By the time I had reached the beach, the kayaker was sitting on the grassy strip above the stones, so I crossed the beach low down near the shoreline, from where I could give him a wave of acknowledgement without being within earshot. The smooth slate-grey disks of the beach were too small to step from stone to stone, but had no purchase on one another, so they slithered about under my feet as if they were constantly trying to turn my ankle. They squeaked and clattered like a shaken bag of childhood marbles. I knew I must have looked clumsy and graceless. The mere presence of an observer had returned me to self-consciousness. The great gift of solitude is that although you might think that it provokes introspection, actually the very opposite is true – you can lose all sense of self. A stranger in the distance was all it took to change my perspective, so that instead of seeing a landscape, I saw myself within it.

The rock platform at the foot of the cliffs was not quite level; in places it was on a tilt so that only its seaward edge was dry, and it had captured vast quantities of seawater and presumably rainwater too so that it was filled with rock pools a foot or two deep. Some of these were enormous, the size of swimming pools. Rock pools make for a challenging habitat, where the temperature and salinity of the water varies wildly. These were packed with life regardless, and I paused for a while and peered in through the clear water at a miniature, apparently self-contained world of its own. There were little copses of sea lettuce and red seaweed amongst which darted tiny fish – blennies, I thought – and transparent prawns with waving antennae. There were colonies of sea anemones gently waving at me, and winkles grazing on the algae. Looking through the skin of the water was like looking through a glass at an alien world.

In places the cliffs fell away, and the landscape opened up, sloping gently up into the hills. There would be raised beaches partway up the hillside, and the ruins of crofts, sometimes solitary, sometimes in groups that formed ghost villages. The clearances had taken place over a hundred and seventy years ago, and the crofts had not weathered well. Walls only a foot or two high remained, sometimes little more than a footprint. These crofts were tiny, single-roomed affairs; they seemed impossibly small for a dwelling-place, and I wondered if some of them might just have been for storage or for use as shepherds' huts. I sat inside the void of one, a place that someone might once have called home, and tried to imagine what life could have been like here, but it was impossible to put myself in the crofters' place and see this land through their eyes; it was a language that I did not speak. Beside each croft was a little patch of land, often with the remains of a boundary wall. These fields were correspondingly tiny, pocket handkerchief-sized, but they had been carefully tended; levelled and cleared of stones so that even now they held a growth of fresh green grass rather than ragged heather. From a distance, this chequerboard of small brilliant green patches was more visible than the ruins of the crofts, and showed the meticulous care the crofters had taken over the land they had been ejected from.

I came upon a cleft in the cliffs, where the two walls of rock suddenly turned inland and faced one another across a narrow dark ravine. As I approached, there was a flurry of life as a raven burst from its nest just inside the mouth of the ravine. It flew up, calling in alarm, and settled on the clifftop close by, hunkered down with its neck feathers all puffed up in a ruff, trying to make itself bigger, shouting at me in annoyance. It bobbed with each croak, like a cat trying to cough up a fur-ball. Within seconds its mate flew in, circled low above me, and perched on the facing clifftop, so that the two of them were on either side of the entrance close above me, like guardians of the gates. I looked from one to the other as they each tried to drive me away from their nesting site, and then I noticed something that gave me pause. Beside one of them, amongst the heather on the cliff edge, was what appeared to be a skull, with its two empty orbits staring straight out to sea. It didn't look like the skull of a sheep or deer; it had a high domed forehead, like a human skull. I felt that I had no choice but to investigate, and started to make my way closer to the ravine, much to the increased annoyance of the two birds. As I approached, though, the skull deformed and elongated, like the skull of an alien. It was an illusion, an unlikely white rock with two black holes that made it look like the perfect image of a human skull.

The raven is the most mythologised of creatures. In the Icelandic 'Edda', the two ravens Hugin and Munin, representing thought and memory, sit at the shoulders of Odin, and each day they fly out to report back on the world of men, while Odin waits for their return, anxious that they will abandon him. To the natives of the Pacific Northwest, such as the Haida and the Tlingit, the raven was a trickster god, responsible by deception for the creation of the world. Often, their association is with death and bad omens; as carrion feeders they are depicted as intermediaries between life and death. Edgar Allan Poe's raven was 'grim, ungainly, ghastly, gaunt and ominous'. And yet, although I had just been faced by the absurd coincidence of coming upon a wild raven perched alongside what had at first sight appeared to be a human skull, I had felt not the least trace of alarm. I supposed it must stem from all the time I had spent among ravens at my home in Wales, where they were my neighbours, my constant companions, and so I could not see them as being charged with any symbolic weight at all, but only as fellow creatures, intelligent and with their own dark beauty.

One more substantial headland lay between me and my destination, and as the day was wearing on, I decided to climb the hill and cut a corner inland rather than following the rocks. My route led me onto a bare moor of grass and heather, and I soon began to wonder if my sense of direction would hold, or if I would inadvertently drift away from the sea and range too far inland. I felt that I had gone far enough and when I came upon a stream, I decided to follow the water down, as the safest course. A sudden waterfall dropped into a hidden hollow in the moor to a reedy tarn where seagulls bathed. By the waterside a small herd of red deer hinds grazed. They raised their heads at my approach, then trotted casually off up the hillside, glancing back at me to check I was not in pursuit. One remained behind, and allowed me to come much closer. She walked slowly, deliberately, after the others, broadside to me so she could see me. At her side, always touching her flank, was her calf, trying to keep up with her on overlong, wobbly legs. This was the very beginning of the calving season, and deer can walk from birth. I wondered if this could even be baby's first steps, and stopped in my tracks, so as not to panic them.

Red deer had been rather elusive so far on my walks in the Rough Bounds, though on my winter journeys at least, the train journey over Rannoch Moor had passed through a vast congregation of them, hundreds if not thousands. Arguably, the red deer is no longer entirely native; just as our wildcats have hybridised with domestic cats, our red deer have mingled with the closely related sika deer, introduced here from Japan and East Asia. It sometimes begins to feel as if the entire natural world is actually our own creation; an unforeseen consequence of our inveterate meddling.

I am not a purist about these things, though. I would never argue that we should automatically eliminate anything that we have introduced, and bring back those we have destroyed. Undoing matters is itself another attempt to manipulate the world. The brown hares in our fields have been here long enough now that they have earned the right to stay, even though they have been partially responsible for driving our native mountain hares into the remotest fringes of their original range, just as the grey squirrel has driven out our native red squirrels. In Ireland, where the brown hare never reached, the Irish hare – the local variety of the mountain hare – lives quite as happily in the lowlands as the uplands, and has entirely abandoned the habit of turning white in winter. The red deer, across much of its range, was originally a creature of the forest rather than the hill. We have created a new reality, and we can hardly undo the past when we cannot even put a stop to the declines of the present. Our first priority must be to safeguard what we have left before it is too late. As for biodiversity, so it is for climate change; we cannot make things better until we have found a way to stop making things worse.

I made my way back down to the shore and continued along the rocks until I finally saw the white strand I had been aiming for. There was a single small tent on the beach. I was not surprised to see it there; an hour before I had been picking my way around a narrow ledge on the cliffs when I saw the kayaker I had spotted earlier out on the water, slipping methodically through the calm water. It seemed a very serene way of exploring this coast, compared to my trek. I had presumed earlier he was likely headed for the same beach as me, but doubted there would be much chance of my getting any further ahead.

The strand was in a small sheltered bay, a perfect arc of white sand with a little stream running through it and a rock jetty to either side. Two rocky islands in the mouth of the bay sheltered its waters; this was why sand had been able to collect here. Far away across the sound I could see the long peninsula of Ardnamurchan, out to the lighthouse at its tip, the westernmost point of the mainland. The bay teemed with life, compared to the rocky coast which had offered a parade of oystercatchers and fluttering rock pipits in the main. A ringed plover scurried along the sand ahead of me, and terns plunge-dived into the clear shallow water. There were the heads of swimmers out in the bay too – the dog-like heads of seals; the grey seals of these wilder shores rather than the harbour seals I had watched in Loch Sunart. A flotilla of eiders bobbed in the water; handsome birds in crisp black and white, with their distinctive steep foreheads and smudge of pastel green. They were all drakes; the ducks would be out on the islands, tucked up in eiderdown. A black guillemot flew low across the bay, jet black, with a crisp oval patch of startling white, and a crimson gape and feet; a bird of primary colours. Puffins get all the press, but I have a particular fondness for the black guillemot. While the other members of the auk family such as the puffins, common guillemots and razorbills nest in vast, noisy colonies, black guillemot pairs will go off alone to find a quiet nook of their own. They are solitary birds, like me.

I walked over and introduced myself to the man on

the beach; he was indeed the person I had seen earlier. I told him I didn't think I had time to move on and leave him in peace, but I would pitch my tent at the far end of the beach, behind rocks and out of sight, and I offered to help him carry his heavily laden sea kayak up the beach to save him dragging it. Here was someone else who organised his life in such a way as to allow himself the freedom to seek the wild places. He worked the boats, four months on and four months off, and most of his free time he spent in the Cairngorms, where he lived. He was a volunteer assessor for a group of inner-city youngsters on a sea-kayaking expedition as part of an award scheme. I worried briefly that we were about to be joined on the beach by a party of teenagers, but he had gone on alone; they and their instructor would not make it this far today, and would camp a couple of miles back along the shore.

When I admired the spot we had both chosen for our camp he told me of an even more spectacular beach an hour or two further west. He always used to aim for it but it was easier to reach from the road-head than our camp, and had become too well-known, too busy for his liking. For all the welcome he had given me, which had even included the irresistible offer of morning coffee, this was clearly a man who liked his solitude. He decided he should go and check on his charges, and so I ended up having the beach to myself for the evening. I took a small bottle of malt whisky and my field glasses and clambered out to the tip of the rocks at the edge of the bay. There I found a perfect observation post, a cleft in the rocks where I could sit back comfortably and look out over the waters, as if I was on a throne of stone.

Out among the rising heads of the seals were diving birds; three of them. They had thick bills, grey heads, chequerboard backs, and zebra-striped breasts. Black-throated divers, in their full summer regalia. This bay must have been full of fish, with the seals and divers all diving repeatedly and successfully. The last time I had seen them in summer plumage had been half a lifetime ago, in a favourite Swedish lake. It was not a particularly large lake, but it was deep into the woods and had to be approached through the trees. This meant you could arrive entirely without being seen. There was a single islet topped with a half-dozen Scots pines, at the top of which perched a huge osprey nest that had evidently been extended each year until it was the size of a hay bale. A pair of divers nested here, and their unearthly wails drifted across the water, giving the place an extra layer of magic.

Another pair of divers flew into the bay. They can seem graceless and cumbersome in flight; they fly low to the water, and their feet trail behind them. Divers are designed for the water; their feet are set far back so they are ungainly on land, looking as though they are always about to tip onto their bellies. These new arrivals were not more black-throats, however; they were our other nesting diver, the red-throated, with long pale grey necks, a splash of crimson on their breasts, and brilliant red beady eyes. Both species are scarce breeders, and on these islands are found almost exclusively in the Highlands. It felt like a great privilege to have five of them in close proximity at the same time. Strange-looking birds, beautiful but otherworldly. With their small heads but great thick necks for swallowing fish whole there is something reptilian about them, for all their elaborate plumage.

The sheltered waters of the bay were smooth and mirror-calm, unmarked save for the ripples from the diving birds and seals, but suddenly a wave rolled in; a single low wall of water like a tidal bore. I looked back to see where it might have come from, and there at the tip of the island something big and black and snub-nosed rose from submarine depths. It was a whale, with a thick backswept dorsal fin, and a blunt 'melon', the swollen forehead that it uses as a sonic lens for echolocation. It paused on the surface for a moment and then dramatically rolled onto its side, crashing down on the water and sending out another wave. Then a second whale rose alongside it and did the same before they both sank into the deep water. These were not true ocean giants but pilot whales, smaller but still impressive, almost the size of a killer whale. I thought I had lost them, that they must have swum behind the island, but then one rose again in exactly the same spot, and again. It was impossible to know how many there were, but I repeatedly saw two or three rising together, and estimated that this must be a pod in double figures. As I watched, transfixed, I could see there was a method to what they were doing. In the midst of them was a circle of water that was white and wild, churned into chaos. They had made a trap, had surrounded a shoal of herring, and were engaged in a feeding frenzy.

Pilot whales are not inshore animals; they spend their lives far out to sea at the edge of the continental shelf, but they are known to follow prey inshore, and are prone to occasional strandings as a result. I had spent many hours sitting on beaches all over the world, and yet I had never seen anything quite like this. In fact I had never seen whales in British waters before, and always imagined that if I ever did it would be from the bow of a boat. Their show continued for over an hour, though it felt like one frozen moment, out of time and place, something that could never be forgotten, as the huge mammals roiled in the waters of the bay. After a while they had company, too; dolphins, drawn in by the commotion, leaping in pairs over the waves churned up by the whales, giving the impression that they were doing so out of sheer joyfulness. They were not the more familiar bottlenose dolphins that often come close to shore, that I had watched all over the world, that I had even swum with – not by intention, but because I happened to be in the water when the dolphins came by. These were the more decorative short-beaked common dolphins, that normally live out in deep water like the whales, and that were undoubtedly camp followers. They were elegant creatures that looked tiny alongside their gigantic cousins, with a splash of pale yellow on their sides and racing stripes. I felt unreasonably privileged to be here, to experience the joy of seeing them, so completely unexpected, in this remote little bay. It felt like a gift.

When my fellow beach dweller came paddling back into view a little while before sunset, I was still sitting out on the rocks. I told him about the whales, and he said he had just been watching an otter along the shore, and it had allowed him to come surprisingly close in his kayak. I decided to walk a little way along the shore to gain a better view of the sunset over the Small Isles. Dazzled by the sun as it dropped towards the horizon, I stopped to listen to a cuckoo that was calling, loud and clear and bell-like. It is such a far-carrying call. I was reflecting on how a single calling bird can fill a whole valley with its repetitive chant, on how it is so often heard and so seldom seen, on how it is actually far less common than you might think, when I saw it sitting on a rock about ten feet away from me, and found myself almost embarrassed by the sheer wrongness of my musings; it hadn't been far away at all. I watched it for a while as it posed for me, flicking its wings. Cuckoos are such odd-looking birds; their wings too low, their tails too high. They look as if they have been assembled out of spare parts, a Frankenstein's monster among birds.

This bird seemingly wanted to add injury to insult, for it woke me the next morning at the very break of day. I peered out of the flap of my tent and watched it as it flew back and forth over the sands of the bay, calling over and over, with a long trail of pipits strung out behind it in close pursuit, like the tail of a kite. And I forgave it; in fact, I felt fleetingly sorry for it. It must be confusing to be a cuckoo. The pipits were the closest thing it had ever known to parents; they had been its constant, its tireless providers. Then it had flown off to Africa for its annual holiday, and when it returned home, they wanted to drive it away.

My colleague on the beach came by to fill his kettle at the stream that ran by my tent, and we had morning coffee together. We discussed nature writing, of which he was something of an enthusiast, and then went our separate ways, one by water, one by land. I followed the coast around the head of the peninsula until I finally made it back to the road-head on the north side of the Rhu. There I shed my load, hiding my pack under a clump of gorse, and headed into the village for supplies. It was only about an hour each way into the village, though I was hobbling now, with my wet foot a mass of blisters. A family of greylag geese floated on the calm waters of Loch nan Ceall in a row, six fluffy goslings in the middle, and the parents alert and watchful front and back, like a protection detail. On a little island close to shore, a half-dozen harbour seals dozed in the sun. A group of trainee kayakers was out on the water with their instructor, and one of the seals caught up with the party to investigate, popping its head up alongside each of them in turn.

I had chosen a site for my new camp that was very different from the previous night's wide-open expanse of sand and sea. Here at the mouth of the bay were little nooks of weedy beach hidden in niches along a coastline of ragged rocks. I tried walking barefoot along the beaches, but they were not sand, and were entirely made of tiny shards of what looked like coral that dug into my feet like broken glass. These so-called coral beaches of the Highlands and Islands are not actually made of true coral at all, but maerl, species of coralline red algae that grow without roots on sandy seabeds, forming beautiful branching nodules of calcium carbonate. The mouth of the harbour was filled with low rocky islands, dozens of them, which overlapped one another so that there was no view of the open sea, and the waters of the bay were freakishly calm. There was a channel of still water perhaps two or three hundred yards across between me and the islands, where seals and eiders bobbed.

I found a small level and sheltered patch of turf backing onto one of the beaches. I brushed away the carapaces of crabs left by feeding otters, then pitched my tent and went out to sit on the rocks for the evening. The water was so still and clear that I could see right to the sea floor, with whole forests of kelp gently waving in an undersea breeze, and between them little flocks of darting fish. As the evening wore on the midges came out to play, the worst so far, and eventually I was driven back to my tent to zip myself away from them for half an hour.

Later, a light sea breeze picked up, and I was able to emerge again. The sun was setting behind the islands, and a swan was flying in low, straight towards me. Even from a distance I could tell that it was not a resident mute swan but a whooper. It is strange how two birds that look so alike can feel so very different; the mute is stately and serene while the whooper is wild and restless. It should not have been here. The whooper is a winter migrant; just a few pairs stay to breed each year, on the Shetlands and Outer Hebrides. Perhaps this bird had been injured and was unable to cope with the arduous flight back to the Arctic tundra, and had stayed on alone, waiting for a mate that would never come. As its path crossed the headland, it flew right above me, perhaps twenty feet away, and I could see the distinctive lemon yellow of its bill. It looked down at me and whooped three times; a call that sounded full of yearning, the call of the wild.

As the light began to fade, an otter appeared on the rocks and slipped into the water. It swam straight out from the shore, and beneath the glassy water I could see its whole body, every twist of its thick tail. It created the strange illusion that it was swimming through air, floating just above the surface of the sea. It did not dive or hunt but headed purposefully towards the islands opposite. Eventually it was so far away that its head was just a pinprick, leaving a little v-shaped ripple that followed it. And then, finally, it swam into the trail of light as the last rays of the setting sun spread across the face of the waters, and winked out altogether.

September

The Kingdom of Crows

The miles ticked away in darkness. I would already be in the Scottish Lowlands by the time it was light enough to see. I don't find it easy to sleep sitting up on a crowded train; it is more a matter of snatching a few minutes at a time. My head lolls, my neck stiffens, my legs cramp. And on this journey, when I dozed off, my heart would cramp too, so it became an even more uncomfortable and restless trip than normal.

The train arrived in Glasgow at breakfast-time, and I walked the short distance from Central to Queen Street. This was basically the halfway point; the journey from Glasgow to the Rough Bounds would take as long as the journey from the south coast of England to Glasgow. The streets were full of people rushing to work. I began this last leg of the journey reading a book, but as the train climbed into the Highlands, the landscape quickly became a distraction that I found impossible to ignore, and I spent the next four or five hours just looking out of the window at the increasingly dramatic landscape. It was afternoon when I arrived at the ferry port in Mallaig, and just a short wait for the boat. There are big ferries that head off to the islands, to Skye and to Rum and the Small Isles, but I was taking the little ferry across Loch Nevis to the village of Inverie on Knoydart. There are two boats that make this crossing, depending on the time of day; a smallish ferry, or an even smaller one that carries nine passengers only. The boat doesn't just transport people; it takes everything – building materials, food supplies, mailbags. Nothing can make it to Knoydart by road, for there is no road. Everything was piled high on pallets on the deck and then covered in tarpaulin in case it was a splashy crossing.

We left the little harbour and set off on the half-hour journey. The weather was mostly overcast but there was not much chop. I spent the journey as close as I could get to the prow of the boat, looking out for the harbour porpoises that arced away, slick and oily, from the boat as it approached. I counted eight in all: two pairs, and then a group of four. These are the smallest members of the whale family and usually tend to avoid boats, unlike the dolphins which will often ride in the bow-wave, so there were probably more that I missed. It was a better showing than the last time I had been out in these waters, when I had seen just one pair. There had apparently been a party of bottlenose dolphins in the vicinity, and the porpoises had made themselves scarce, for dolphins predate on their smaller cousins.

I had chosen my night's campsite before we had docked; a small, isolated strip of sand tucked behind a rocky promontory, a beach that was not even marked on the map and well away from any trails. It looked almost certain to be somewhere I would have to myself. So when we arrived at the jetty and disembarked, while all other passengers turned towards the village, I set off in the opposite direction, and followed the shore. The south-facing slopes of Knoydart, all around the village, are perhaps surprisingly thickly wooded. It is not entirely natural woodland, but is nevertheless a very attractive mixed wood of large mature trees that must once have been estate woodland planted in Victorian times, and is now well managed by a community trust of local residents.

As I followed the shore west, a buzzard flushed from the trees and flew low ahead of me between the tree trunks, then swept up to perch again a few trees further ahead. As if it was leading me on. The sun came through the clouds, illuminating the heather-clad hills above. The heather was in full bloom and the rowans were laden, heavy with berries. At first there were a few loch-side houses, widely spaced along the shore, but then I reached the end of the last track. I circuited a shallow bay that cut deep into the land. A wren appeared in the bracken along the shore, calling at me. Such a bold little creature; it allowed me to approach to within just three or four feet, and in spite of my presence it threw back its head and burst into song. For such a small bird, the wren has a powerful voice, and is one of the few birds that can still occasionally be heard singing in the dead of winter. When I lived in Wales, I remember once hearing one in full song while out walking on Christmas Day. The hunting of the wren is a Celtic midwinter tradition, with the wren perhaps being symbolic of the year just ended. After that Christmas it became something of an annual ritual for me, my own version of the wren-hunt, to go out after each winter solstice listening for my first winter wren. No wrens were harmed in the making of my own personal tradition. But no more. Never again will I mark the turn of the seasons and the lengthening of days with birdsong. The wren had just joined my ever-growing list of birds whose song was now beyond my reach. It was so close, I strained towards it, hoping to pick up something, even a single low note, but there was nothing there, just the breeze blowing. It was gone for good.

I regret the loss of the song of the wren because I can recall it, in full throat on a frosty winter's morning on a Welsh riverbank. I do not miss the calls of birds that I have never heard, and I do not miss the ultrasonic calls of the bats that lived in my Welsh loft, because they were ultrasonic; they were always beyond my reach. Our view of the world is strictly limited; by our place in time, by geography, by our scale. And it is constrained by the operational limits of our sensory organs. When I see a rainbow, I am seeing just a segment of the wavelength of light; other creatures might see a quite different rainbow. I am keenly aware of the decline in numbers of some of the birds and animals from my childhood forays into the countryside – the corn buntings and skylarks and water voles – but I do not mourn the absence from those fields of the corncrake, at least not in the same personal way, for the corncrake had already gone before I arrived. Its passing belongs to the childhood memories of an earlier generation. The world we grow up in becomes our blueprint for what is natural. Changes that take place more slowly, over the course of more than a single human lifetime, will always fail to register in the same way, because every new generation creates its own new normal. Dramatic changes in population sizes, deforestation, loss of habitat and climate changes; all are happening on our watch. We have brutalised and compromised the world far more fully than may be readily apparent. We need to think beyond our own time span, to the time of our children's children and further, for nature's sake as well as their own. The natural world surely has an intrinsic value which goes beyond its utility to us as a resource.

To reach the spot where I had seen the little beach from the boat I would have to mount a high ridge. It was steep-sided; I had to scramble up the slope using my hands to haul myself up, first from birch trunk to birch trunk, then from heather stalk to heather stalk. It was hard work with a pack on my back that had to include enough food for several days as well as camping equipment, but it felt good to be off-trail. Then I had to cross the marshy hilltop, hoping that my guess was good. My concern was that I would reach the shore and wouldn't know whether to turn left or right, but my aim was true and as soon as I mounted the last ridge I could see the little beach right below me. There was a dome of rock, almost an island, out on the waters of the sea-loch, linked to the land by a low spit of turf, with on one side a rocky beach, and the other a strip of white sand. I clambered down the steep hillside and shed my pack on the close-cropped grass. Someone else had camped here once; there was a circle of stones from a long-ago campfire. The grass was littered with flotsam, tangles of fishing net and floats and inscrutable nautical plastic. I took off my boots and stepped onto the sands. There was a thick coil of seaweed at the very top of the beach; this beach would disappear entirely at high tide. I walked down to the water's edge and waded in. The sun was breaking through the clouds and further up the loch towards the mountains it was showering; there was a rainbow reaching across the waters, my own personal rainbow.

My intention had been to camp on the sandy deer-cropped turf, but as day turned to evening an onshore wind began to pick up from the west, steadily gathering in force until it reached a point where it would not be easy to put up my tent. But in the lee of the almost-island was a cluster of contorted birches clinging onto the rock face, and beneath them a small level grassy shelf which would suit me perfectly. The only thing this place lacked was fresh water; I found a few rainwater pools among the rocks above the splash zone, but the water was brackish and unpalatable. I regretted not filling my water bottle when I had crossed streams earlier in my walk. I had just a couple of mouthfuls left; that would have to do until morning, for it was too late now to go on a water-hunt. I was never a good planner; I cannot count the number of sunsets I have watched during my travels only to find myself lacking food or water or firewood or shelter and having to either make do without or go to a great deal of trouble to remedy these errors of omission. It is a kind of chronic optimism that is my downfall. I will come to a stream and wonder whether perhaps I should top up my water bottle, and will think, no, there is sure to be another stream closer to my destination. And I will repeat this pattern until I have missed my final opportunity. I have got many a soaking from the same flawed logic. I have been out walking and it has started to rain, and I have wondered if I should put on my rain gear, only to decide it will be a shower, bound to stop shortly. And so it is that I seldom put on my waterproofs until it is really far too late, for I am already soaked through.

After pitching my tent, I sat on the outermost rocks and looked out over the loch. This promontory was an otter midden; there were carapaces of crabs by the dozen, and large fragments of the strange rough orbs of sea urchin shells, in beautiful symmetrical patterns like mandalas. A team of gannets criss-crossed the loch, hunting. It is impossible to mistake a gannet for anything else, even at a great distance. While seagulls may appear perfectly white, they are dull against the radiant whiteness of the gannet. Even under an overcast sky, gannets seem glaringly brilliant, as if they have a ray of sunlight shining down on them. Following the pack was a solitary Arctic skua, hook-winged and predatory-looking. The skua is a pirate. It will wait while other birds, generally terns and gulls, catch themselves a fish, and then it will pursue them, mobbing and harassing them relentlessly until they surrender their prey. I was not sure I could imagine a skua taking on a gannet, though; gannets are powerful birds.

I knew that I was ill, but had decided that the risk to my health was most likely not severe enough to make me think twice about coming. I understood that my journey would become far more of a physical challenge than it would normally have been, but I was determined to complete this project anyway. In times like this, I always seemed to find untapped reserves of stubbornness that I could draw upon. I avoided telling people of my difficulties, or telling anyone where I was going, even my children. Apart from anything else, I wanted to have the freedom to roam, not to stick to a preordained plan, and I knew that I was aiming for places where I would be unreachable. This may seem rash, but I was determined that no one should feel any sense of responsibility for my intransigence. This was my problem; I saw no reason to make it anyone else's. Sitting alone on the last rock on the shore, I felt I had chosen solitude and emotional self-sufficiency perhaps more completely than ever before. It made me feel more alone, more independent. My body might be failing me but it somehow made me stronger rather than weaker, more sure of myself than ever.

It was over three months since I had last been here. In part, I had wanted to avoid the peak tourist season, but I had also wanted to be available while my younger daughter was off school for the summer. My older daughter had returned from several months in Southeast Asia, her own first independent travels. She had come home seemingly more grown up and enthused; she talked about wanting to come walking in Scotland with me. Another time, I said; this is something I have to do alone. We did all go camping together over the summer, however, as we almost always have. They brought friends with them, and it was a wildly different experience from my solitary ventures. It was all about the company. Now that September had come, my older daughter had gone off to start university. When a child leaves home it is, of course, a watershed moment for anyone, and although my younger girl was still at home, I did wonder if I was in some way having to prepare myself psychologically for times to come, when I would be alone whether I liked it or not.

Looking out to sea, I could watch dark heavy clouds blowing in from the west, fast and low, lower than the hilltops. The clouds reached down, ropes of rain, tentacles that stroked the surface of the loch. I waited until the first one hit me; a sudden blast of cold wind-lashed raindrops. Remembering that I had left the contents of my pack spread out on the beach, I sat it out and waited for the rain to pass, then far too late gave in and ran to throw everything in the tent before it was all soaked through.

I was woken in the early morning, not by cuckoos now, for they had all flown back to Africa, but by hooded crows calling in the birches that overhung my campsite. These birds are the northern equivalent of the carrion crow, and are closely related, even occasionally inter-breeding in the Scottish lowlands where their ranges meet. For a long time they were believed to be varieties of the same species, but more recently the hooded crow, the corbie, has been upgraded, and it is now considered a species of its own. Studies have shown that given the choice it will prefer to pair with a crow of its own type, and there are behavioural differences too; while the carrion crow is usually seen alone or in pairs, the hooded crow is more inclined to gather in small groups. I unzipped the fly of my tent and looked out. The crows flushed, calling in annoyance, and alerted a group of three red deer hinds that were picking their way down the hillside, presumably heading for the green turf above the beach. Seeing me, the deer paused, then abandoned their descent, turning along the coastline and picking their way across the rocky slopes like mountain goats.

Having no water, I did not want to wait around, but packed up quickly and headed along the shore. Out on the loch was a low rocky islet. It was barely an island; it was so low that a high wave would have swept over it, but in this watery place that was half-land, half-sea, the grey seals had gathered in numbers. Unlike the alert harbour seals, these animals were supine. Their blubber drooped over the rocks so that they looked like outsized drops of spilt candle wax. I sat and watched them all doing nothing together until the rain began again, and I sheltered under the best available nearby tree for a while until I could no longer dispute that it had set in, and dressed in my rain gear. I headed back in the direction of the village and as I walked the rain grew steadily heavier. No shortage of water now.

There were few people about in the village. There was something about this small row of loch-side cottages that made it feel qualitatively different from the other villages

I had travelled to on my journey through the Rough Bounds, and caused it to seem more remote than it really was. Knoydart once supported a sizeable population of crofters, perhaps over a thousand, but then they were pressed by the landowners to vacate the land. Most chose to emigrate, and set off for Canada, and those that stayed were eventually forcibly removed in one of the most notorious incidents of the Highland clearances. For a long time the entire peninsula was almost entirely uninhabited save for a few estate workers, and it is only in recent decades that the population has slowly begun to build up again, though still only to a tiny proportion of its earlier levels. Everybody here has consciously chosen to isolate themselves from the world, to live in a small community cut off from the mainland. Everybody is an incomer, even the Scots who live here. No one is here by accident, and no one is passing through on their way to somewhere else, for it is on the way to nowhere.

The village had a single pub, a post office, a shop and a café. I went into the café, stripped off my rain gear and hung it up. Soon I was sitting amidst a small pool of water in which floated bits of bracken. Outside the window, the sun came out over the loch. I ordered a coffee and apologised for dripping everywhere. I told the guy at the counter that I had been walking in the rain for two hours, and the moment I stepped inside the rain had stopped, and the sun began to shine. He said, that being the case, then perhaps I should stay all day. I asked him how long it would take to walk over the top, to the north side of the peninsula, as I was thinking of spending a couple of nights camping over on the virtually unin-habited north. He said he had only done it once, with a group of friends. It had taken them six hours, but they had been partying, drinking as they went, so I would probably do it in less. This was all I needed to know; I could make it to the other side before darkness fell.

I wondered what it would be like to live in such a remote place. All the people settled here must at some point in their lives have responded to its very isolation. They could hardly be here by accident. I presumed that in season there must be as many visitors to the peninsula – hill-walkers and summer visitors – as there were full-timers. But living here year round may not be a solitary affair at all; quite the opposite. It is normal enough in the city to have no idea who your neighbours are, yet in a small community like this everybody would know everybody else, and would have some degree of inter-dependence. It would actually be rather a social affair, I thought. The quest for solitude is less about choosing a remote location than it is about striving for an emotional self-sufficiency.

The lure of the cabin in the woods is something that speaks to many people, but it is often interpreted as a negative desire; the desire to escape from social commitments and pressures. When I tell people about my years of solitude in Wales, they will often respond by asking what it was that I was running away from. But it never felt like that, not to me. I was never running away; always running towards.

I set off out of the village and uphill through the woods. There was a well-worn trail all the way to the other side as this was very much walking country, but nonetheless from the moment I left the village I was not to see another soul for over twenty-four hours. Generally I prefer to break my own trail, but it was already midday and it was not a short walk, and there were three-thousand-foot mountains between me and my destination, so an alternative route might not be so easy to find. A broad steep track led through a mile of woods before breaking out onto the open moor. I found myself walking up a long valley at the bottom of which was a gushing river. A herd of long-horned shaggy highland cattle blocked my way. They had the run of the mountains but had chosen to stick to the path, just as I had. They were completely fearless and had no desire to move out of my way, so I had to wind between them and push past them. As the trail rose it closed on the river, until eventually the river was right alongside the path, rocky and fast-moving. It gushed from a hidden loch, right in the middle of the peninsula, which suddenly came into view, guarded by a solitary ruined cottage. A little rowing boat was chained up at the water's edge, and the fish were jumping. I sat in the sunshine in the lee of the ruin and imagined what life might have been like in such a lonely spot. It was a beautiful prospect. This was not a tiny mountain lochan but a significant little body of water for so high in the hills – it would take perhaps twenty minutes to walk it end to end. Behind the cottage the hillside sloped sharply up towards the summit of Ladhar Bheinn, the highest mountain of the range, and across the water, where there was no trail, the slopes were flanked with birch woods that seemed to pour down the mountainside. At the head of the loch, a tangle of waterfalls flowed down from the invisible hilltops above. And I could see into the future – about two hours into my future, I guessed – for I could just make out the trail ahead, rising with alarming steepness into the hills beyond and over the ridge between two mountains.

The trail as far as the loch had been a broad gentle ascent; easy walking. But this was another matter, a narrow mountain trail that ran with water. After the heavy rains of the morning, the rainfall had found the path of least resistance, and walking the track was like walking the bed of a stream. It was not so bad where it was rocky beneath, but where it was soft underfoot the path disappeared into a mire of mud and flooded moor-grass, and I had to watch my feet at every step, and sometimes leave the path altogether. The trail became progressively steeper and more arduous as I ascended, and I found myself regularly pausing for a breather and taking in the view, looking back at how far I had climbed, and trying to work out just how much further I had to go before I reached the summit.

The pass was only fifteen hundred feet high; nothing really. In the Andes – in Ecuador, Peru and Bolivia – and in the Himalayas – in India, Nepal and China – I had readily crossed passes ten times this high, though on those occasions I had admittedly started my walks from far above sea level. As I struggled my way towards the top now, I started counting my steps. A hundred steps and I would reward myself with a momentary break. I had to admit I was not in peak physical condition. Though I was not a youngster any more, I was in pretty good shape and had always prided myself on my resilience. It should not have been this hard. It made me feel as if I was at a much higher altitude when every step feels like wading through water, or as if gravity has unaccountably increased.

On the ridge above me stood a stag. I thought it curious how often I saw them like this, silhouetted against the sky; no doubt because I often missed them altogether when they were camouflaged against the background of the hillsides. This one was unmissable; a fine strong animal with a magnificent head of antlers, perhaps as many points as I had ever seen before. It was alert, watching me with interest. I thought that it would drift back out of sight, but it must have decided that I was no threat, for it continued its way and came closer.

Behind it came a long trail of hinds; I counted them over the ridge, sixteen in total, quite a harem. This stag would have a fight on its hands when the autumn rut began, but it looked well equipped to hold its own.

I made a final push for the top, and suddenly the summit cairn appeared. A pair of ravens flew up and circled, calling, and their deep and sonorous voices echoed across the hills. They flew out over the valley I had just ascended. Beyond them the loch that had seemed so big as I passed it looked tiny now. I smiled to see them. My friends the ravens; I shall never lose them, they will be with me always, until the very end.

It does feel almost as though I have a special affinity for the crows. They always seem to be there, a part of my life, mostly in the background but sometimes taking centre stage. I remember the sweltering summer of 1976, when it was too hot to do almost anything, when all that the rest of my family wanted to do was lie on a beach. Each day we would drive out to Pagham in West Sussex where the beach was less crowded. While my family sunbathed I would walk out alone along the spit towards the mouth of the harbour, where there was a colony of beautiful little terns, tiny and yellow-faced, nesting in their scrapes on a gravel island. As I walked the path one scorching hot day, the air flexing in the rising heat, I saw a crow walking the path ahead of me. I kept expecting it to flush as I approached, but it never did; instead it hopped up and perched on top of my head. I felt strangely proud as I continued my way towards the harbour with my animated headdress. And then it drove its beak into the very top of my skull, as if it was trying to crack a nut.

In Wales when I walked in winter on the moors I would usually see only crows and ravens; almost nothing else remained. In the early spring, as early as February, when the ravens were the first bird to breed, I would watch them almost daily at their nesting site. Along with the snowdrops, they were the very first signifier that the world was still turning. And there was the injured raven that I cared for, briefly, until it recuperated.

I remember a Himalayan base camp, where the ravens stalked and scavenged, as proprietorial as cats, as if I was just a guest in their domain, which I was. Above all, I recall the crows of Zimbabwe, and one of the most surreal wildlife experiences of my life. I was hiking in the Chimanimani mountains in the Eastern Highlands of Zimbabwe, hard against the border with Mozambique, which was in the midst of its fifteen-year civil war. After hitching to the road-head, I spent the remainder of the day heading up to the mountain refuge. It was not far, not as the crow flies, but it was a ridiculously steep route; the path ahead was like staring at a vertical wall reaching up to the sky.

It was worth it, though. The refuge had a fine prospect east from its verandah, over a broad lush river valley to the long chain of summits running north–south beyond. There would have been room for twenty easily, but I was the only one staying there that night. Tourism was at a low ebb, and those few who did come were mostly just visiting the game reserves. Behind the refuge was a stone basin for washing in rainwater, and a sign that warned you to beware of the crows, for they would steal your soap if you left it out.

In the morning a solitary waterbuck was wading knee-deep in the lush grasses of the valley water meadows. Its pale rump looked like a bullseye, a target for predators that said; bite here. I dropped down into the valley and forded the stream before making my final ascent to the summit of the range. It was a strange alien landscape; these mountains were deeply eroded, layered with contorted stacks and pillars of pale bare rock, sudden caves, and the unfamiliar botany of the African mountains. Though I spent the day in sunshine, the final summit was blanketed in cloud. When I finally made it onto the broad stone dome at the top, I stepped into a thick mist. *Kraa*, a voice called; *kraa, kraa*. The peak of the mountain was covered in crows, dozens of them, obscured by the fog. They didn't seem to want to leave the summit; they stalked away from me on foot, and only flew a few yards at a time, if at all. These were Cape crows, bigger than our own carrion crow but smaller than a raven, with longer legs and a more slender, curved bill. They each paced through the fog cartoonishly, looking more like a caricature of a crow than a real-life bird. I walked on through the swirling mist towards the topmost point of the dome, the crows parting ahead of me, and then I saw the sign at the very top ahead of me. It was a tin billboard, with a row of crows perched on top, creaking at me in warning. This sign marked the international border, and informed me that under no circumstances was I to proceed beyond this point. The sign was full of bullet holes. It was a strange otherworldly place, like a kind of Gothic purgatory, here in the kingdom of crows.

Dropping down from the fogbound mountain top and back into sunshine was like returning to the real world. That evening, when I returned to the mountain refuge, I had company: a group of Zimbabwean women had arrived and were cooking up *sadza*, mealie-meal, over a log fire, and invited me to join them. After we had eaten, darkness began to fall, and the stars to appear; the unfamiliar constellations of the southern hemisphere that made me feel a long way from home. We sat out on the verandah and they pointed them out to me as they appeared: first of all the Southern Cross, and there, hovering above it, Corvus, the crow.

Night Music

I had imagined that when I reached the summit cairn at the top of the pass I would be able to see across the entire width of the peninsula, from Loch Nevis to Loch Hourn, or from loch heaven to loch hell, which they supposedly translated to from the Gaelic. I didn't know how Loch Hourn had earned itself such a bad name; perhaps I would find out. Most likely it was a simple matter of geography; these northern shores consisted of steep north-facing slopes reaching down from high mountains, and would be in shadow for much of the time, perhaps in winter for almost the whole time. The settlements alongside Loch Nevis, meanwhile, faced the sun and would be bathed in light for the whole of the day. The view I had anticipated was not to be, however; the lie of the land made it impossible. The peaks rose steeply to either side of the path down from the pass, so it was like walking down a steep gulley, or the floor of a canyon that twisted and turned, and I would not catch my first glimpse of the loch below until I was almost halfway down.

The journey downhill was a lot easier than the journey up; there would be no more need for rest breaks. In fact I had to constantly remember to pace myself down the steep slope. My knees would thank me for it later. I had once spent a whole day of rapid descent thousands of metres down the Himalayas, ten hours in all, which led to an uncomfortable night with my knees throbbing in swollen regret. On the lower slopes of these hills lay great swathes of pine wood, a scattering of venerable pine trees. They were thick-trunked, broad-backed and twisted with age. They made me realise how the woods of North Morar that I had previously visited were very much secondary growth. I knew I wanted to pitch my tent beneath the shelter of these great trees, but it would not be easy to find a spot. The woods remained here, while they had been stripped from almost everywhere else, for precisely the reason that the location was too remote for human exploitation. Not only were these wooded slopes and dark north-facing hillsides far from habitation, they were also very steeply pitched. Finding a level, sheltered spot would not be easy.

The path down to the loch passed beneath the woods, so I left the trail and turned back up towards the hills, following the gulley of a raging burn that came crashing down the mountainside in a series of cascades, a miniature valley perhaps twenty or thirty feet deep that had been gouged out of the hillside, and was hidden from view, like a secret. There I found what seemed to be an ideal spot. Beneath the shelter of two of the greatest of the pines, and right alongside the biggest of all of the waterfalls on the hillside, was an unexpected level space the size of a room, soft with grass and moss and studded with a profusion of chanterelle mushrooms. This was perfect. I congratulated myself on having stumbled upon such an ideal situation. I would just pitch my tent and then I would prepare food and sit on the biggest of the jumble of boulders at the foot of the falls, my little bottle of single malt whisky in my hand. There is nothing like the sound of falling water to promote perfect, mindless peace. For me, in my condition, with my aching heart and my reserves of energy run down from lack of sleep, it had felt like an arduous day's walking, and I was looking forward to an evening when I could just kick back.

It was not to be. As soon as I began to set up my tent, the midges descended; the air was thick with an endless black biting mist. The season generally ends in September, with the first frost, but that had not yet come. The summer had been warm and wet; perfect conditions for a frenzy of midges. I threw my tent together as quickly as was humanly possible, and dived in. There would be no sitting by a waterfall soaking up the peace, for there was no peace. Hundreds of midges had made it into the tent with me, either blown in during the few short seconds that the fly sheet was unzipped or clinging to my clothes. But at least hundreds felt like a manageable, finite number, rather than the swarms outside. I kept unzipping a tiny spyhole to look out, as I hoped when darkness fell they would drift away, but they were still there in their swirling millions. There was nothing to be done but to lie there and listen to the roar of the waterfall right outside, the waterfall of tranquillity that felt as though it would remain for ever just out of reach.

That night I lay awake for hours in the darkness of my tent, plagued by biting insects and with the roar and gush of the waters just a few feet away. And behind the erratic crash of the falling waters was another sound, a constant low drone like the sound of a distant plane taking off; the background sound, I supposed, of the entire burn, a whole mountainside of falling water.

And as I lay, and tried and failed to get to sleep, I gradually became aware of yet another sound, something quite different. I could hear what sounded like a ghostly cello playing, slow and stately, elegant and rather beautiful. I was under no illusion that there was anyone or anything actually there. I presumed it to be the product of some kind of harmonic interference between the rush of the falls and the background drone of the waters. I wondered if I could entirely be imagining it, but then concluded that, really, all sound is a creation of the mind, the brain's attempt to make some sense out of external cues. It was not just in my head, I decided, at least no more so than any other sound really exists only in your head; I was convinced it was actually there, a natural product of the environment. It did not alarm me in any way; rather it felt comforting. It was a simple musical refrain that lasted for ten or fifteen seconds, and then was repeated from the start with minor variations, over and over. If I'd had more knowledge of music I would have been able to record the musical notations. I supposed that it was site-specific, tied to the very spot where I had chosen to lay my head, and that if I moved a few feet it might well change, or disappear entirely, and on another day when there had been a little more rainfall, or a little less, it might be lost too. It was a song of the earth, my own personal song of the wild, and for all the failings of my hearing I was undoubtedly the first person ever to have had the privilege of hearing it.

I rose at first light, keen to be on the move and away from that tiny confined space filled with biting insects. I peeked out but the clouds of midges were of course all still out there waiting for me, so I put together a day bag as quickly as I could and made my exit. I scrambled up the twenty-foot-high bank, pulling myself up by the jumble of pine roots, and then stopped. The mist had settled in the night. It had sifted through the old ragged pines to make the landscape look raw and primeval. The mountain tops were clear, and so was the valley; the fog had fixed itself halfway up the hills, so that each hillside was wrapped in a long white scarf that undulated like a frozen wave. The air was completely still, not even the faintest trace of breeze, so that the mist hanging between the trees was utterly motionless. There was no sound at all, no movement, as if time itself had stopped dead and I was walking in the suspended moment. There was an eerie hush, and I drifted down the hillside as if in a dream, as if I had stepped out of the real world.

My route down to the loch-side took me past a bothy with three silent tents pitched outside it. In half an hour's walking I had seen no living creature, not a bird in the sky, nothing that moved. But if I paused for a moment then a cloud of midges would descend on me. It was as though there was no other living creature on earth; just me and the midges. When I reached the shore of the loch the waters were perfectly flat and unmarked. As I passed a headland I saw a pair of mergansers swimming out on the waters. The path in their wake stretched back for hundreds of yards behind them, the only mark on the glassy-smooth face of the waters. I could see the route they had taken for many minutes beforehand. It was like having a window back into the past, and it was enough to break the spell and set time running again.

I followed the shore of the loch along a patchy trail that sometimes clung to the water's edge and sometimes rose into the hills. The landscape was perfect; pine woods and birch woods trailing down the hillside to the narrow sea-loch. In some spots the pine trees hung right over the water; there cannot be many places where these tiny surviving fragments of the great wood reach all the way to the sea. The steep hillside across the water seemed trackless and wild and thick with birch. I would have liked to pause for a while and drink it all in, but as with my waterfall of the night before the midges would not allow it. If I kept moving they could not settle around me, but stopping still was made intolerable. Finally the skies began to brighten and the sun melted away the hanging fog. With the sun came the first tentative breeze, and the great clouds of midges were driven away. I chose my spot and stopped at last to drink in the landscape. I sat on the root-bole of a great pine overlooking the loch, the ground around me thick with generations of fallen cones. I once rolled out my sleeping bag and slept on a soft bed of pine needles, accumulated over centuries and as springy as a mattress, beneath a coastal redwood in Northern California. This pine tree was hardly as grand as that three-hundred-foot giant – few other trees could be – but it was an ancient beauty in an exquisite setting. It was reassuring to think that it had undoubtedly been here since long before I was born, and would still hopefully be here long after I was gone.

It was perhaps inevitable that my thoughts would dwell on mortality and decline. I was suffering with the gripping pains of an as-yet-undiagnosed heart condition. I was fatalistic about it, though. We all get ill, at some time or another, sooner or later. When it comes to our own decline, it is never a matter of if, only of when. And we all have to work within the confines of our own physical limitations. If I could no longer climb a mountain, then I would climb a hill. And if the only thing that was still a walk in the park was an actual walk in the park, then I would find a park. And when the time came that I could do nothing more than look out of a window, then I hope I would have chosen for myself a room with a view worth watching. I had no complaints; I felt privileged and fortunate to have been born in a time and a place where most of the hardships I had endured and wounds I had suffered were in large part the consequence of decisions that I had freely made. I had never been compelled to go to war, and I had never been forced to flee my homeland for my own survival. I'd had the freedom to roam the world without the use of force;

mostly I had been made welcome wherever I had found myself. Generations of people throughout history, and many people now, have had to live out their lives without these luxuries, without peace, without almost guaranteed access to enough food, or clean water, or medicines. My health might apparently be abandoning me, but I was able to be here, sitting under my tree in this most beautiful of spots, and I was grateful.

There was a familiar call, and I looked up. A party of seven ravens flew low above me, all taking turns to tumble, like a circus troupe putting on a show. Ravens usually come in pairs rather than groups, and I presumed this to be a family party. Though they were all full-sized, I took them to be this year's brood, not yet dispersed. Five is a full brood for a raven, so it had been a successful year. Further up the hillside, an eagle soared over the ridge-line and swung in a lazy circle. It was followed by a second bird, and the two slowly swung around each other, looping in and out of view at the top of the crags, circling high over the woods that swept down the steep hillside beneath them. I tried to imagine myself into their place; to see what they saw, to see this world through eagle eyes. They were joined by a third bird, slightly smaller and patched with white. At first glimpse I thought it was perhaps a buzzard out to mob them, but as it closed on them and followed their drifting flight I realised that it was a young bird out on hunting practice with its parents. Golden eagles typically raise just one young each year, if they are successful. It seemed as though everyone was having a good year.

I spent the whole day out walking the shores of the loch, and finally, in the late afternoon, came upon someone else: an Englishman, an ex-soldier with a backpack, walking into the peninsula from the road-head. A long winding single-track road led to the very head of the loch before finally giving out. He was a serious walker, chasing Munros. The Munros are those mountains over three thousand feet high; there are almost three hundred of them in Scotland, and he had less than a score left to bag. The only ones he had left, he told me, were those which were most difficult to access. Knoydart had four of them, and he would summit them all in the next few days. It was a very different, goal-oriented approach to the hills from my own. Such a methodical approach is just not in my nature. I would not have the stamina to do what he was doing, or the drive. I was quite happy to set off and just look and drift about the hills like a circling eagle, in search of whatever sustenance I could find. A little while later, I met a very friendly couple of islanders walking into the bothy and campsite, taking their dog for a long walk; a very long walk. We stopped and chatted, and I was able to give them a report on the state of the trail ahead.

When the afternoon was wearing on, I headed all the way back along the shore of the loch and up to the hills and the woods. I must have walked at least as far that day as I had done the previous day – certainly more than ten miles – but there had been less climbing involved and I had no heavy pack. I had been drowsy all day from lack of sleep, though, which had made me feel semi-detached from the world and made the day dreamlike as I walked past woods and water, beneath sunshine and cloud; it made the idyllic landscape seem almost like a picture of itself, made me feel even more of an observer rather than being truly present.

I did not want to face another embattled night of hiding away in my tent, trapped by the midges. When I reached my campsite, their clouds were already thickening, as if they had been waiting for my return.

So I packed down my tent, gave it a good shaking out, and fled, carrying my things off the hill and down to the bothy. There was quite a gathering there; besides the three people and a dog I had encountered, there were also two pairs of Scotsmen, lean and battle-hardened hill-walkers. Everyone was my own generation. The tourist season was over, the students were back to their studies, and the place had been left to those like me who could not quite leave these hills alone, and approached them with dedication. It was a very social night, by my standards anyway, as everyone told tales of the hills and of their travels. Between us we had seen a lot of the world. Though my visits over the course of this past year had all been solitary, I could not help but note that those that I had run into had without exception been friendly and welcoming. Everyone had a shared appreciation of this land; we all understood exactly why we would want to be just here, for all its discomforts and inaccessibility.

After darkness fell, people settled early. Everybody else had pitched tents outside, so in the end I bunked alone in the bothy, taking the opportunity to hang all my damp things to dry and to spread myself out. I had a

good restful night of it, a night very different from my
night by the waterfall.

I had to retrace my steps over the peninsula and back
to the ferry if I was to make it home. The only alternative
would be overland through tens of miles of uninhabited
wilderness, and would take days, days that I did not have
to spare. And I did not trust that I had the strength. The
return felt less onerous than the outbound journey,
however. Outward bound, it is unclear what challenges
lie ahead, or how long the journey may take, but when
retracing steps it is a known quantity. I knew that the
crossing was readily manageable within the hours of
daylight, without my having to push myself, and so I
could take my time over it.

The next evening, camped out on the strip of grass
that backed onto the sands, just beyond the splash zone,
I fell asleep to the lapping of waves and the muttering of
geese out on the shallow waters of the bay, but I was
suddenly awoken a couple of hours later. It was pitch
black and there was a crushing pain in my chest,
something nameless pressing down on me, something
invisible, formless, like dark matter. I fumbled about in
the darkness of my tent, feeling for where I had left my

nitro, and took a gasp, but there was no obvious relief. Getting back to sleep now was not an option. I would have to get up before light anyway, to pack up and get to the jetty in time for the little morning ferry. I could not afford to miss it; I had to get home in time for a hospital appointment. My original plan had been to come here a little later in the month, but then the appointment had been set and I had decided to move things forward, for fear that my consultant would admit me straight away, or at least urge me to scupper my plans, tell me not to be so foolish.

Knoydart is undeniably remote, and was perhaps not the most ideal of places to come for someone with a rapidly escalating heart condition, but what was I supposed to do? Lie on the sofa with a TV remote in my hand? My condition was not typical, anyway; I could climb in the mountains with a heavy pack all day long with little problem. These episodes always seemed to start when I was sleeping, and were rapidly becoming more frequent and more protracted. It was as if, when I slept, my breathing became too shallow, and my heart was starved of oxygen. It was as if I was relaxing myself into an early grave. I had been through something similar before, a decade ago. That time it ended in surgery, twice. Heart disease runs in the family, and you cannot argue with heredity; all you can do is learn to accommodate it.

I unzipped the fly sheet of my tent and stepped out barefoot into darkness. I took another hit of the nitro spray; damn but my chest was hurting. The grass was cool beneath my feet. Three paces and I was standing on sand. I decided to take a walk along the strand. I could not see a thing, but it was a beach, there was nothing I could bump into, nothing that could possibly go wrong, apart from the one big thing. The night was mild and the cloud was low. The waves were gentle and the geese had settled down for the night; there was no sound save for the occasional peep of a restless oystercatcher. There was no moon at all; it is not often that I find myself in the presence of such near-perfect darkness.

Beneath my feet I felt the crackle of dried-up wrack, the sharp jab of a razor shell, the unexpected cold soft touch of a stranded jellyfish. I was relaxed, almost unnaturally so, if a little hesitant about what was to happen next. I had made my choice, and now I must take the consequences. This was the point at which I should have been calling for an ambulance, but there was no ambulance, there was no calling, there was just me, alone in the dark on a beach, remote from all help.

A breeze began to blow in from the sea, and after a while the clouds above me parted to reveal a patch of starry sky, and I looked upwards into the great silence. I found the square of Perseus, I found the skewed W of Cassiopeia. It felt somehow urgent that I tracked down what I was looking for. I triangulated between the stars until I located the faintest smudge of light. I see you, M31.

M31 is the Andromeda galaxy, or at least the bright core of it – most of it is too faint to be seen without a telescope. It is one of the only things from outside our own galaxy that can be seen with the naked eye; the only one that I have ever managed to find. The tiny droplets of light that hit my retina set off on their journey two and a half million years ago, before man was born. I imagined some remote pre-human ancestor knapping stones together for the first time on the African plain, and beetling his brow, becoming dimly aware, with an awareness that has no words, of a potential future. Yet while it is so very, very far away, Andromeda is still our nearest neighbour. It is near enough that, while galaxies across the universe are all accelerating away from one another, Andromeda and our own galaxy are wrapped in each other's gravitational embrace, and will one day merge to become one. Those few photons of light that somehow managed to reach me formed a tentative link between a barely imaginable past and a completely inconceivable future. It may not be an original thought to remark that looking at the night sky can help put things in perspective, but for me, right then, it really did.

There is a certain pleasure in walking in complete darkness; as if every step is a step into the unknown. As a child I would go out alone onto the downs, close my eyes, and run full tilt while counting out loud. Each time I would try to count a little further, while fighting against the temptation to count faster and faster. There was only one time that I ran headlong into a tree. I walked the strand all night, until the darkness began to have texture, until the first grey light of dawn. The pain in my heart had not gone away, but nor had it got worse. I was still here. The onshore breeze had picked up, and brought with it a sudden squall of rain. In daylight I would have seen it coming; the low cloud sweeping in over the loch, the tendrils of rain reaching down to the surface of the waters. I paused and turned towards the sea, spread my arms, turned my gaze to the heavens. Bring it on. Ice-cold raindrops lashed against my face; it felt like being alive.

OCTOBER

Autumnsong

Though it was only a month since I had last been here, things had changed vastly. The woods of birch and oak were in their full autumn leaf; all yellows and oranges but not yet ready to fall. They looked exquisite, painterly. The purple heather of the hills was gone now, but the moor-grass had faded from the lush green of my last visit to a whole palette of earth colours; yellow ochre at the tips, burnt sienna at the base, and umber at the root, so that the hills looked scorched by the fires of summer. The first snows had already fallen on Ben Nevis but the sun was shining. Great flocks of redwings and fieldfares had arrived from Scandinavia, drawn by the glut of rowan berries. The scattered flocks were so vast that they might take several minutes to pass overhead, and then they would suddenly tumble from the sky as they came to another rowan. I could hear the chatter of the fieldfares, but the redwings were gone to me. These birds were ravenous, plundering the land like Viking marauders.

Every time I came to another rowan tree, unseen birds would fall from the branches one by one at my approach, dropping out of it before rising. It seemed astounding that one little tree could hold so many birds that were invisible to me. Every time I thought that must be it, they must all be gone now, another group would pour out of the tree's hidden recesses, and the ground beneath the rowans would be slick with their spillage.

Deep in the woods, I was surprised by a sudden peal of birdsong; the autumn song of the robin, one of the few birds other than the wren that sings almost the whole year round. I sat and watched it singing to the world, and wondered if I was hearing its whole song or just a sample of its lower notes, or if perhaps it was just that this song is like an echo of its full spring song, with less variety, less range, than the full-throated melodies I had listened to from all the robins singing on the shores of Loch Morar back in March. Either way it was enough to delight me, out of season in a year which had held so little song for me. The robin is one of the few birds that hold a territory throughout the winter, for it cannot bear the company of others. Its call is the auditory equivalent of a 'keep out' sign, or a challenge to all comers. It sings because it wants to be alone. And yet our subjective response to the natural world has a kind of validity of its own even when it bears little relationship to reality. There is certainly something very moving about a solitary bird singing into silence at year's end. After the vitality and exuberance of spring, this is a bird that will not let go. It sings on amidst the falling leaves, it sings on as the nights draw in, it sings on as all about it falls quiet. This bird's song may not have the sheer brio that it had when the year was young, but it has subtlety and a seemingly elegiac, thoughtful quality. It sounds like the voice of experience, and I cannot fault it for its tenacity. When all else has given up, it just keeps right on singing; I am still here. No surrender.

I had come almost on the spur of the moment for one more visit, tempted by a weather forecast that had promised an unexpected dry week, and even some sunshine, not at all what you would expect at the end of October. I had largely been lucky with the weather all year. My motivation for avoiding the peak tourist season had been driven primarily by a desire to keep away from the crowds, and have the best chance of being alone, but locals told me that the summer had been a washout. In July and August the weather had been biblical; it had rained every day for forty consecutive days. And so I had thrown together a bag and jumped on a train. After my stay in hospital I was heavily medicated and somewhat dazed as a result, but it had been established that my own peculiar back-to-front variant of angina was provoked not by exertion but by rest. There was nothing to stop me climbing a mountain; in fact, there was a better argument for me to climb, and keep climbing, and never stop. There was no possible response other than stoicism to an ailment that followed its own path so resolutely and so independently of any of my actions. In fact, it was quite liberating to be told there was nothing I could do about it, for I would not be faced with a hard choice between my health and my lifestyle. No compromises required.

I had decided to try my luck at a little bothy that I had stumbled upon back in May. I was relying on my luck, and the fact that the season was now over. I had no plan for what I would do if it was fully occupied, for I had failed to pack a tent. Coming upon a bothy by accident while roaming in the wilds seems like a perfect way to find one; they are, after all, intended as an emergency shelter in a remote place rather than as a destination in themselves, and for this reason they are not publicly advertised but exist more as an open secret for those in the know, so they are not inundated and over-exploited. While a proportion of them are maintained charitably by the association, many are on private land and exist on sufferance. If people take advantage, leaving litter or damaging the local environment, they could easily be lost. They exist on trust.

I had been following the coast far from the road when I saw a little shack perched on a stump of rock overlooking the sea; perhaps a boathouse, I thought, perhaps a bothy. Though it was still early afternoon, I thought that if it was a bothy and was unoccupied then perhaps I could spend a night there and make it my temporary home, drop off my things and use it as my base for the rest of the day while I explored the nearby coastline. It was an odd location, certainly not built for convenience, as I had to clamber up the rocky pillar to get to it; it had more the feel of a lookout post than a habitation.

It was not unoccupied; inside were two Scotsmen, sitting in a fug of smoke from their roll-ups and with a bottle of whisky between them. They invited me to join them, and I was happy to shed my load and cool off in the shade for a while, for it had been hot walking. They had both spent the previous night here, and as it was already well into the afternoon they looked settled in for the day; neither of them was about to move on. They had not arrived together; both were habitual solitary wanderers like me. But they were old acquaintances, having met before over the years in other bothies far away, and had some catching-up to do. I had no intention of staying now that I knew the place was in use, for I had come to be alone, but I was interested to chat to them. These were members of my tribe, I supposed, fellow travellers, and it would be fascinating to compare notes, to see to what extent their own motivations matched mine, and perhaps gain a greater understanding of what drives us.

The older of the two men looked a little weather-beaten. He was coming down off a five-day bender, he said. He lived in Glasgow, and when he was home he never went out, never drank. He saved all his drinking for the Highlands. As soon as he had saved a little money he would be off again, hiking and staying in bothies. He had been coming to this particular bothy for fifteen years. In the early days he had hardly ever seen anyone else here, but more recently it had begun to get better known. The last time he was here about a dozen people had turned up and pitched their tents nearby. It had been quite a party. I got the impression that although he had no problem with his own company, he also had no problem with his solitary excursion turning into an unexpected social event.

The younger man appeared to have no home. He said he was thinking he would soon have to start looking for work again. It would be live-in work, bar work or kitchen work, anywhere in the Highlands and Islands. He would settle for a while until he had a little money saved, and then take off again, going from bothy to bothy, hiking every day. He reminded me a lot of myself when I was younger. He told me he might possibly head on later today, to another place a few hours down the coast. I wondered if he was saying this out of consideration to me, to let me know that it was fine for me to stay if I needed, for it was a tiny place, with space for only two to sleep. Most bothies have been built from the reconstructed shells of abandoned crofts or farmhouses, but this one had apparently been purpose-built back in the fifties, which explained why its location was more scenic than practical. It was a single room the size of a large shed, with bunk space for two, a stove in the corner, and a single window that looked over the sea. The best TV in the land, the older man said. He picked up his field glasses. That boat has been moored there for hours, he explained. He looked out at it and said the guy was diving for scallops, there were a lot of scallops there in the bay. Then he named the boat, the fisherman, and the village he came from. OK, I said, now I'm impressed.

I was not planning to stay; it was early still and I was going to head along the coast and find a beach to pitch my tent on. The older guy told me there were some decent caves along the headland, too. We sat and chatted about the various bothies we had been to, and the characters we had met along the way. They were certainly more experienced than me – it seemed as though they could have written a Michelin guide – but I was able to name a couple I had stayed in that were new to them. I told them about my place in Wales, that I had spent five years living on my own in a cottage with no services at all. Like having your own private bothy, they said, and I suppose it was. I had never really thought of it quite like that. I was surprised when they both said that they couldn't do what I had done; it was too much, for too long. The older man seemed particularly put off by the fact that I had cooked over a log fire for all those years. That was too much trouble, he said, though I assured him that you got used to it, so much so that it became second nature, as easy as cooking on a stove. But he liked his comforts, and appreciated the fact that at home in Glasgow he had a twenty-four-hour shop just on the corner. It seemed ironic, given that he had spent fifteen years coming out here to get away from it all, but I suppose I had to accept that I was an outlier, and there were no rules. There are many people who are drawn to the world's wild landscapes, but not all of them will be chasing solitude. Many will be happier with a companion, or a group of friends or family, someone to share the experience with. But wherever you go in the world you will find a rump of people who walk alone, by choice rather than by necessity. It cuts across race and class, and if historically it has been culturally more difficult for women to assert their independence in this way then this is changing, as more and more women reclaim the right to break their own trail.

Though I had not known of the existence of this particular bothy, I did know of at least half a dozen or so others scattered across the Rough Bounds. I had passed one before in the distance; there had been a couple of people sitting in the doorway and two or three tents pitched nearby. It made me realise that I might have to rethink my plans a little. I had thought that I might stay in a bothy from time to time when it suited me, but it seemed clear that they had become better known and more popular than I had remembered from previous visits to Scotland. Almost every one I had visited in the past I'd had to myself. But they are well placed, often about a day's walk apart, so they create their own destination, their own routes. If I wanted solitude I would be better off picking my own path, just wandering, and pitching my tent wherever I might find myself. It crossed my mind that I had perhaps done things back to front; that it would have been better to have resorted to bothies on my winter visits, and left them to others in season. Perhaps I would return in winter, find myself a bothy, stoke up the fire and remain there for a few days.

I said my goodbyes and clambered down off the rocky perch and onto the beach. We speculated that we might very well meet again; another time, another bothy. They had been very hospitable; if I had felt at all uncomfortable stepping into a room of strangers then they had quickly put me at my ease. I walked along the top of the beach towards the cliffs.

So now that the summer nights had gone, I had returned. I could still have camped, but the first frosts had come, and sitting by a driftwood fire in a bothy seemed like a more appealing option for someone who was not at full physical strength. The little rocky stack was poised between two curved beaches of grey stones, the bothy sitting low-slung at its summit, small as a shack, half-hidden amongst a tangle of stunted, weather-beaten oaks. No smoke emerged from the stovepipe that protruded from one corner. I picked my way up the rocks and between the scrubs of oak and unbolted the door. I need not have worried; there was no sign of anyone else having been there for days, at the very least.

I dropped my pack and looked out from the one window. The place had been built so it faced out to sea, looking above the topmost branches of the oaks. The view was almost entirely of the waters of the bay; you would have to come close and turn your head to see the shore to either side. There was the stove, a bench to sit on, a wooden bunk tucked into the eaves, a shelf, and almost nothing else. The place made me think of an anchorite's cell in its austerity, and in its setting, too; poised high on a rock face on western shores, facing straight out to the ocean, away from the world of men.

Now that I had shelter, I needed just two more things: firewood and water. There was a bow-saw standing in the corner, and I had seen a whole tree washed up on the beach, so I walked down and cropped its branches and roots until I had sufficient for the evening. It was a tiny stove, so only small pieces of wood would do. I was annoyed that, as usual, I had not thought to fetch water on my way in; I could see on my map that the nearest stream was a good way along the coast, and on these trackless shores the return journey might take me the best part of an hour. There were still a couple of hours before dark, though, so there would be no harm in having to devote a little time to it.

The shore was ragged and broken, with promontories that rose and fell in a tumble of rocks and led out to a scatter of islands, and held tiny hidden bays and beaches. There was no sign of any trail; if I was not hopping from rock to rock I was climbing and descending steep ridges that were chest-deep in dying bracken. Copses of oak were dotted randomly across the hillside, their trunks and branches contorted and corkscrewed by the elements but their canopies smooth and streamlined by the onshore wind, so that these woods looked moulded to the lie of the land. This was an ancient forest, but in miniature. Few of these trees made it to even twenty feet in height, yet the age of the woods was betrayed by the amount of dead wood, both fallen and still standing. Nothing here had been felled, or coppiced, or replanted; no one had even scavenged here for firewood. They were primeval and beautiful in their autumn colours, though I supposed that they were ultimately dying, unable to regenerate due to grazing pressure.

I found the tiniest stream, trickling through the beach stones of a small bay, and followed it up until I discovered a miniature pool fed by a waterfall six inches high, and filled my bottle. I returned to my perch and got a small fire going. The stove was only small, but it was freestanding and had a metal flue, and punched above its weight, radiating heat that slowly spread from its corner to fill the entire room. I boiled some water on it and made myself a bowl of soup, and then I sat and looked out of the window at the sea. It was hard to look anywhere else; the panoramic view drew the eye.

A pair of cormorants had been fishing in the bay all afternoon, and now they were joined by three black-throated divers in their winter plumage. The two species kept their distance from one another, one side of the bay each. An eagle flew over; a sea eagle, crossing the sound to the far-off hills across the water. And then the seals arrived, and hollowed out the centre of the bay, as if pushing the birds out to the fringes. There were five of them, grey seals, all diving for fish. On land the grey seal looks doleful, and frankly depressed, but here in their element they looked joyful. They would all rise together in a circle, facing one another, their heads tipped back to the sky as if they were roaring with laughter. I imagined them as whiskered old men in a gentlemen's club, telling ribald jokes over cigars and port. As the light started to fade, an otter slipped into the water from the shore of the headland where it had been invisible, unseen, and swam far out into the bay to hunt. Behind it trailed a shadow;

this was a mother and cub. Each time the mother dived, a few moments later her cub would follow. It was strange to see so much without leaving the comfort of my fireside. I could get used to this.

I watched the otters until it was too dark to see, and then I lit a candle and turned my attention to the fire. A driftwood fire, water from a burn, a stone cell; this is all I needed in life. And beauty, I could not live without beauty. I could imagine myself an anchorite, living like this, leading the simplest of lives. I had, after all, spent many years when I was younger leading a life that was not so different from this, and found that it suited me well enough.

On the overnight train I had managed perhaps two hours of awkward sleep, and it was not long after darkness had fallen that I drifted into sleep. In practical terms, it was a mistake not to have forced myself to hold out a little longer, for it meant that I woke hours before it would get light. My candle had burnt down, the fire was out, and the room had turned cold. There was nothing I could do but sit and wait for daylight. I could not take a night walk, for it was a dark and moonless night and having thrown together a bag at short notice I had neglected to bring a torch with me. I doubted that I would even be able to get safely off my rock; I had inadvertently trapped myself. And so I stalked my small cell, pacing out the hours of darkness like a wildcat in a cage.

My sleeping pattern had been compromised by my illness in any event; it is not easy to relax comfortably into sleep when you know that the night could turn to drama at any moment. My nights were restless and my days were spent in a daze; it was as if my waking life and my dream life were starting to bleed into one another. This can be a by-product of solitude too; with no one to draw you back to day-to-day reality the world can start to drift into greater and greater subjectivity. This is why solitary confinement is deemed to be the harshest of punishments. The candlelight flickered against the stone walls and I paced. I had chosen this; it had not been imposed upon me. I was an expert at solitude, with years of practice. I was grounded, secure in myself. This is what I told myself, and I did know from experience that the first night alone is always the strangest; after that I would quickly adjust. There is a moment of transition that you have to pass through, from a social way of thinking to the solitary mind. I checked the time; only another couple of hours before first light. I just had to wait it out.

Wild Heart

For more than half of my life, at home and abroad, I have passed my days in sight of the sea or at least a short walk away. This is no great accomplishment in Britain, an island, but nonetheless when circumstances have kept me from it then I have felt its absence. In my years in the mountains of Wales it was the one thing that I felt was missing, and from time to time the pull of the ocean would draw me down the hill to the roadside where I would hitch-hike to the sea. In between times my most favoured walk was down to the riverbank which served as a substitute shore.

During my explorations of the Rough Bounds I had ventured into the mountains on a few occasions, but more time than I had anticipated had been spent following shorelines. In part the draw was scenic and in part it was because the meeting of the elements was not just a magnet to me but also to a great diversity of wildlife. It had also been a pragmatic choice; as the year had progressed and my health had begun to fail me I had not been physically able to embark on the kind of epic mountain walks into the interior that I had assumed would be the culmination of my journeys around the area.

This fifth journey would be the final instalment of my year of visits; it was eleven months since I had first taken myself to the shore of Loch Sunart. I had expected the unexpected and had found it, though not always in the way I had imagined. I had fallen in love with this landscape and had experienced wildlife encounters that I could never have anticipated in their specifics. This is what I had hoped for, the unrepeatable experiences that are the essence of immersing yourself in nature. What I had not foreseen was the personal journey and the lessons I would learn about myself; I am not normally one given to a great deal of self-examination and the Rough Bounds had been more of a challenge for me than I had anticipated, and had forced me to come face to face with my own limitations.

So on this final visit of the year I thought I should include a trip into the interior. I just had to be sure that I was not overreaching, not being overly ambitious, for caution does not come naturally to me and I had to acknowledge that I was not at full strength. I spread out my map and there in what appeared to be the dead centre of the Bounds was a mid-sized freshwater loch two or three miles long and entirely encircled by mountains. I planned my route; from the head of a sea-loch I would follow a river inland and from the river I would follow a burn up a mountainside and then head over the summit. It was not so far; I could get there and back in a day.

It was a lively mountain river of peaty water but at its mouth it slowed and widened as it reached the sea, forming a tiny estuary of flat grassy islands and a miniature salt-marsh. A little flock of ringed plovers flew up from the salt-marsh as I approached; the inevitable mergansers waited at the river mouth, all facing into the flow of the water, while a solitary swan sailed by, silent and serene. Grey wagtails fed at the water's edge and a pair of dippers bobbed and dived, one on either bank. There was a sudden movement in a waterside birch; a bird of prey spread its wings and turned on its perch on brilliant yellow legs. It was close, and I was surprised I had not noticed it until it moved. It had a dark bandit mask like an osprey, but the ospreys had all left for

Africa. It was just a strikingly patterned buzzard. Every buzzard has its own individual markings; if you stay in one place for long enough you will start to get to know the local birds as individuals.

As I followed the riverbank I got too close for comfort and the buzzard lifted off, mewling. A second bird flew out of the trees and joined it and they circled each other above me. Or rather, they spiralled around each other rather than circled, for each turn took them a little further upriver, and it struck me that if I had been able to map their flight paths they would have formed a double helix. I followed beneath them, walking away from the loch towards the hills. This was evidently a fishing river; there were signs marking the limits of different reaches, indicating where you could or couldn't cast your line. In places there were even park benches, which looked bizarrely out of place in such a wild landscape, and I sat on one for a while just because I could, because it was there. But today there were no fishermen. This was not an inaccessible valley; the road and the railway line ran along the same valley as the river for the first part of my journey.

After a couple of miles the river was joined by a burn

that headed straight down from the hills and this is where I crossed over the road and under the railway line and aimed for the wilds. The burn raced down a steep wooded gulley while the path followed alongside on the open moor. Great torrents of fieldfares and redwings gushed overhead; I had never seen such multitudes of winter thrushes. They had flooded in from the north-east and as the winter wore on they would disperse southwards but for now they were held here by the great harvest of berries.

The trail climbed steeply for an hour or so and the valley floor disappeared from view. No more river, no distant sea-loch, no road or railway, and the very last of the few houses of the valley were gone too; I could see nothing but the scorched yellow moors and the mountain tops. It was not an easy ascent for me but the narrow trail winding upwards was distinct enough, and the weather held, cloudy but dry. Then I mounted a ridge and the path dropped into a bowl surrounded by hills and filled with peat bog and peat hag, the source of the burn. I lost the trail almost immediately; this wild land absorbed everything. My boots sank deep into the wet soil but if I paused to watch I could see my footprints disappear before my eyes. If I were to lie down here I would sink slowly into the peat until no trace of my passing remained. I would be perfectly preserved as the seasons turned, and would never be found, or perhaps I would be excavated in some distant future, mummified in the frozen moment, and some remote descendant, perhaps no longer even human, would wonder who I was and what I lived for, and my tanned leathery smile would tell them nothing.

Occasionally, mounting a heathery hillock, I would come upon a thin trail and think for a moment that I was back on track, but the only footprints I found would be the slots of deer, and I finally had to accept that if there was a visible trail then I had long since parted company with it, and I would have to make my way with just a general sense of direction as my guide. I was lost in the wilderness. The wilds of the Scottish Highlands may be insignificant in scale when compared to the vast expanses of northern Canada or Siberia, but when you are on foot and have lost your way, they can feel quite big enough, and wild enough. Every year hill-walkers go missing in these mountains, and not all of them are found. I had seen a 'missing person' sign earlier that day. It marked the last known location, six months ago, of a man exactly my age who had set out on a five-day walk into these hills and had not been seen since.

It was bleak and lifeless up here; not a single crow was in the sky and there was a complete silence. I climbed a ridge over the bog, hoping that I would be able to catch a glimpse of the loch and recalibrate my sense of direction, but I saw just more of the same and dropped back down into another bowl between the hills. It was then that I heard a sudden loud roar, close by, other-worldly and shocking in the emptiness. I looked all around me but could not find its source. It is an in-evitable consequence of having only one functional ear that I have no sense of direction, when it comes to sound; everything originates from the same place. If an acquaintance spots me in the street and calls my name I will likely spin around in a complete circle to find them, much to their bemusement. There was another answering roar, a little further off, and then it was as if a chain reaction had been sparked, for the hills all around me reverberated with roars and bellows.

I realised that I must have walked into a battleground; that the rutting season of the red deer had begun, and these unearthly calls must be stags. Although I was completely surrounded by them I could not see a single one; they were all hidden from sight just beyond the ridge line.

There was no alternative; I would have to go up to go down. To find my bearings, I set off up the mountainside to higher ground. Otherwise I could spend the whole day wandering in these wastes, walking in circles and getting nowhere. This was the right call, for I had not climbed so far when I got a sudden glimpse of blue far below. Though it was a long way down it was close. I had not really been lost at all, I told myself; I had been on track all along. I started to make my way down the steep scree slope, walking sideways on the loose rocks as you do, to check my descent. And then I came to the edge of a crag, poised high above the loch. I followed its edge until I came to a place where it peaked to a point, a spectacular overhang that soared precipitously over the valley. It was a spot so dramatic that it looked as though it belonged in the Sierra Nevada rather than the Scottish Highlands. I inched my way out to the very lip of the overhang; it was irresistible.

Loch Beoraid was sprawled out beneath me, almost

entirely enclosed by sheer mountainsides. At its foot there was a break in the hills, and the loch gave way to a couple of smaller lochans and then the river Meoble that led their overflow through a valley to distant Loch Morar. Peering over the edge of the cliffs, I could see down to the golden canopy of a spectacular wildwood of birch that led all the way down to the water's edge.

I skirted the crags until I found a way down into the almost impenetrable woods. The hillside beneath them was entirely covered in a jumble of giant boulders, many as big as garden sheds, all covered in a thick carpet of mosses and with sprays of ferns springing from every crevice. There were hidden ravines, hollows and caves, and the boulders lay against one another in improbable balancing acts. And in the niches between the stones grew the ancient trees. The birch of these parts is the downy birch rather than the silver birch of more southerly climes. The silver birch is a slender tree with branches that droop decoratively and which is short-lived; its lifespan is on a human scale. These trees were made of sterner stuff. In spite of their obvious similarity, they were much more rugged in character. They were twice as tall, twice as stout, and much more ancient. They can cope with higher rainfall and wetter conditions. They are the trees of the far north.

Woods seem to have a personality all their own. I don't just mean the difference between species – say the difference between the dark tangled mystique of a yew wood and the sculptural elegance of a beech hanger – I mean that an individual wood can have some intangible quality that makes it stand apart from all other woods. This one somehow felt different from the other birch woods I had travelled through. The birch is part of a natural succession. It is quick to take hold, and it will usually be the first tree to grow on neglected land, before finally giving way to oak or whatever other tree forms the climax vegetation of the locality. Here, it was a permanent fixture. Nothing else would ever take its place; it was as though it had finally been able to step out of the shadows, out of its role as supporting act, and fulfil its true potential.

My progress through the woods was unbelievably slow; it was hard to imagine a more uncompromising terrain. Almost the whole time I had to use my hands as well as my feet as I tried to find a way between the boulders, using root and branch as handholds, clutching at handfuls of crumbling moss. I constantly had to backtrack as I found myself at another impasse. I imagined that this place must have been just like this since the retreat of the glaciers and the return of the trees; ancient, unchanged, and utterly inhuman. And although I knew that even these woods were inevitably in jeopardy, that they would never be able to regenerate and colonise the wider hillside due to grazing pressure from the uncontrolled deer population, I felt that I had finally found something I had been looking for. This was the wild heart of the Rough Bounds, a place that was pristine and without surrender, a place that I felt I deserved, because I could never belong here; I could only ever pass through.

It was still a good couple of hundred yards down the steep hillside to where I could see the waters glinting below, between the golden leaves of the trees. I guessed that it might take me the best part of an hour at this rate, bouldering from rock to rock. I stood on a carpet of moss and found that it was growing on air. I flailed, trying to find some purchase, something to grab hold of, but found nothing, and began to slither and tumble downwards. I fell about ten feet or so, and must have somehow rolled as I did so, for I came to rest head down in a crevice between the rocks, with my things scattered all around me. I was soaked through from landing in sodden moss, I had barked my shin and bruised my elbow, and I had a gash on my cheek just below the eye from where a branch had caught me on the way down. But it could have been a lot worse. If I had broken a bone I would have been in a fine mess indeed, for I was a long way from anywhere. I never plan for the worst, always assuming that everything will work out just fine. This incorrigible optimism has stood me in good stead, for it has given me the freedom to lead a life more adventurous, but I have always known that it could one day come back to bite me. This was life, I supposed; one minute you could be standing heroically on a cliff edge, staff in hand, master of all you survey, and the next you could find yourself upside down in a muddy hole.

I decided to tack sideways through the wood, and make my way down to the loch-side over open ground; I had been following a route that was almost impenetrable in its intransigence. The edge of the wood was marked by a deep ravine with a little stream at the bottom. It was extraordinary that such a tiny stream should have created so deep a gulley, but I supposed that it must have its moments after high rainfall when it turned into a raging torrent. The crags above the wood, the ravine to its side, the chaos of boulders that it grew in, the loch at its foot; all conspired to cut it off, to make it a world apart. I was sure that the deer could get into it with a little determination, just as I had, but was equally sure that these flukes of geography that had made it so inhospitable and so awkward of access were just what had preserved it in such a pure state.

I picked my way cautiously down into the gulley and then diagonally up the facing slope, to where I was on easier terrain; a grassy hillside with scattered trees. I followed the hillside until I once again had a fine prospect over the entire length of the lake. Far away, perhaps a mile or so, was the inevitable wooded island. I imagined hauling a canoe over the mountain tops and paddling out to it. I am told that further north of here there is a large island in a loch that has its own small loch within it, and that loch too has its own small island. An island on a loch, on an island on a loch. On an island.

The view was of mountain and crag, water and sky, wildwood and island. There was no road, no trail, no human habitation. There was just one mark of human intervention visible. At the foot of the loch, where it and its associated lochans turned to river, was a small dam, with a shed beside it that I supposed was a small hydroelectric power plant, and a trail that led along the riverside towards it. It was only a tiny affair, not big enough I thought to affect the water level of the loch, but it was enough to remind me that there is almost nowhere that we haven't tampered with. I recalled a visit to the Gearagh in Ireland's County Cork. Here, the river Lee left the hills and spread over a broad flood plain, and a great oak forest grew on low muddy islands surrounded by shifting channels of the river, in an impenetrable inland delta, a kind of temperate Okavango. Alluvial forest such as this is an incredibly rare habitat, with only a few examples worldwide; it grew from the retreat of the glaciers, and survived for ten thousand years in one of the few countries to have suffered worse from deforestation than Britain has. In the 1950s, just a lifetime ago, a hydroelectric dam was built on the river, the forest was felled and the plain flooded.

The Gearagh is a strange otherworldly place now. A broad valley flooded with shallow water, out of which protrude thousands upon thousands of blackened stumps. A fragment of the forest survives, perhaps ten per cent of its original extent, and I spent the day walking its bounds. It was just enough to give me an impression of what had been lost.

It had been mostly cloudy all morning, but now the day was starting to clear. The eastern sky was a glorious blue, with just a few small clouds dotted in it, while above me it was still thick with a straight-edged cloud bank that stretched from horizon to horizon, north and south. And this sky was reflected in the waters below. The far end of the loch was a tapestry of blues, of reflected hills and glints of sunlight, while directly down the hill beneath me the waters reflected the roiling clouds above. These reflected clouds should surely have looked twice as far away as those above me, but somehow the waters seemed instead to bring them closer, to shrink distance, so that it felt as though I could reach down and grab them by the handful. I considered that the extraordinary beauty of this spot was as much in the moment as in the place itself; that I could visit this loch a hundred times, and ninety-nine times it would not look quite as spectacular as it did right now.

Last Call

The trail from the roadside to the bothy was just a few miles and should only have taken a couple of hours. But I had walked for four hours that day to reach the starting point, first along trackless shores and then along roadsides, so I was already feeling worn out. My failing health made every trail seem longer, every hillside steeper. The path dropped down into dense birch woods where a plank bridge took me over a stream before the beginning of a climb that gradually became more and more arduous. The woods were a riot of colour, of red and yellow and orange and fading green, and were thick with winter thrushes, more of them than ever, streaming constantly overhead.

The bothy had been recommended to me back in May by the two Scotsmen I had met in the little bothy on the crags. This one was popular and better known, they had said, but it had the space to cope with it, and they told me that the setting made it worthwhile. After stumbling upon a bothy by accident, having one on a personal recommendation seemed like the second-best way to find one. With frosts at night, it seemed like a more sensible choice than camping, certainly better than camping without a tent.

The trail was ancient and well marked, mostly stony, but as I made my way up the steep wooded crag-side I managed to lose it anyway, I think when I stepped off the path to circle a tree trunk that had fallen across the original route; and then in the dense cover and the waist-high dead bracken I had failed to pick up the trail again. The problem was that I had not been paying sufficient attention, and was no longer sure whether I was above the trail or below it. Not knowing whether to go up or to go down the hillside, I held my course, in the expectation that I would eventually meet the trail again. Of course this never happened, and yet I persisted to the point where it seemed ridiculous to turn and go all the way back. Eventually I emerged from the woods onto open hillside. I could see down to the shore far below, and up to the tops far above, yet I could see no sign of any trail whatsoever. There was a good reason why the hillside here was bare; it was too steep for trees and I was basically traversing what was almost a cliff. Another day, another cliff, lost again; this seems to be a regular feature of my life. Finally I reached a point where I could not go on, and had to make a choice. I decided to scramble upwards and mount the ridge above me, and having done so I found the seemingly obvious path winding up into the hills. I had wasted an hour getting nowhere, and exhausted myself in the process.

Now that I was on the open tops the path was unmissable; it snaked across the umber moor, twisting between crags, and I could see it stretching out almost to the horizon. Long ago, much care had been taken over this trail, many man-hours spent on laying flat stones over the boggy ground. Although there were occasional muddy hollows that had to be skirted around, it nonetheless had a look of permanence, the look of a trail that was going places. Seeing it wind over the wild moor into the far distance brought to mind the Yellow Brick Road, for all that it was not yellow, and not brick. This uninhabited peninsula had once held three small crofting villages on its outer reaches. For hundreds if not thousands of years, people had called this place home, and generation upon generation of crofters would have used this exact route over the hills to move their livestock.

The sky had cleared and the sun was shining. The trail skirted a pair of high lochans, a sudden glimpse of cobalt blue beneath the hills, and then it was downhill all the way, off the tops and down to the sea. The trail dropped alongside a steep burn that poured down the hillside from the lochs, then over stepping stones and back into woodland. Not birch woods now, but oak, and not the shrunken oaks of more exposed shores; this was a mature ancient woodland of full-sized sturdy trees. I stopped and sat on a trunk and listened out for birdsong, but heard nothing but the mewling of a buzzard. Fallen wood lay everywhere, and I wondered if I should be gathering it for firewood, but didn't know how much further I still had to walk to reach my destination, or whether there would be any source of firewood closer to the bothy.

The trail dropped out of the woods and into a flat river valley. The gushing burn suddenly slowed and wound gently between dense reed beds. Over the tops of the reeds and sedges I could see the bothy on its shore in the distance. Backing on to the dunes was a low turf ridge, and lined up all along the curve of the bay were the remains of a lost village. A heron followed the course of the little river, and a solitary snow bunting blew in from the sea and into the reeds; a bird of the winter, of the far north, with a pure white breast and neck. They normally come in little parties, like drifts of snowflakes, but this one was alone.

I dropped my pack in the bothy and wandered around the ruined village. These blackhouses had long since lost their thatched roofs but were otherwise intact. Unlike the ruined crofts of Arisaig, which left little more than a footprint or a low crumbling wall, these had survived until much more recent times. Lintel stones still hung over their low doors and narrow slotted windows. They had no hearths; the smoke of their fires had been allowed to sift out through their thatched reed roofs, which would have perhaps been held in place against the elements by weighted fishing nets. Though they would have housed entire families, they mostly consisted of a single room. They were well made, though; they had no sharp corners but rather elegant curves of bevelled stone that would have deflected the wind. The inside of the shell of each ruin was thick with brambles, and a wren flew from house to house as I approached. I imagined that the bramble patches of the ruined village formed this bird's entire territory, and it was now the village's solitary permanent inhabitant.

This peninsula had not suffered from the clearances in the same way as much of this area; or at least the impact had been deferred. People forced out elsewhere had gathered here, and the population had grown to unsupportable levels for a place where life was already hard and lived on a very narrow margin. It was poverty that ultimately drove people away. The last house to be occupied was the one that had been converted for use as a bothy. A woman, born here in the village, had lived here alone right up until the Second World War, when rationing, not of food but of candles and paraffin, had finally driven her out. It would be impossible to live in a place like this on one candle a week. I wondered what it must have been like for her, to have had all her childhood memories here, to have been left behind, alone in an abandoned village. Walking the empty village was like visiting the scene of a disaster, yet it had not been a sudden catastrophe; rather, a long slow process of attrition.

Now that the skies had cleared, the weather was

strangely warm for the time of year. I peeled off my T-shirt and walked down to the beach. It was hot enough in the sunshine for it to be sunbathing weather. Over the dunes was a beach of white sand, as fine as dust. The tide was low and the beach was stony down by the sea shore, and thick with mussels. A party of ringed plovers patrolled the water's edge, running ahead of me. The damp sand was a maze of footprints, a perfect record of the whole day's events, waiting for the tide to turn and wipe the slate clean once more. I took off my boots and socks and left them there while I waded the river, pausing to cup mouthfuls of water for quenching my thirst, and to wash. Among the rocks of the low hill at the bay's end was a scatter of scrub and small trees; there would be enough fallen wood for the night.

I returned to the bothy bearing a full load of firewood, all I could carry, and enough to last the night. I had left the door of the bothy open, and as I approached the wren flew out. My neighbour had been visiting. I fetched out the bothy's bow-saw and began to saw up my fallen branches into fire-sized logs.

It had begun to seem as though I would have the place to myself for the night, but not long before dark a young couple arrived. They had cut things very fine; having seen how good the weather was, they had decided on a whim to drive over from Edinburgh. They walked down to the sea to forage for mussels while I clambered up onto the rocks at the end of the bay to watch the fiery sunset. When I returned they were cooking up an elaborate stew on the bench outside the bothy. They were very well equipped. As darkness began to fall and the first stars appeared, a bat flew in suddenly as if from nowhere, and swooped up and down the front of the bothy, twisting and turning low above our heads, so close that I could feel the breath from its wings on my face. Though the couple had not been to this spot before, they regularly headed out to the Western Highlands to find a bothy for the night. We talked of landscape and wildlife, and I spoke of otters. Neither of them had ever seen one, and so I told them that the best time to look for them is after sunset but before dark, or after first light but before sunrise. It is easier to see things when you are alone; you have to remember that two people together make twice as much noise, and that is before you even start talking.

Of course, it is also true that two people double the chances of spotting wildlife. I imagine that what we see is always just a small fraction of what is there; that the vast majority of wildlife sees us, or hears us, or scents us, well before we are aware of it. I like to think of an apparently empty landscape being full of creatures waiting for me to pass out of range. It pleases me to think that there is a hidden world, just out of view, and to create a mental landscape around me that is much more filled with life than it appears. And when I do have a wild encounter, I feel I have crossed a threshold and been granted access to an alternate reality, a world that lives in parallel to my own. There have been many times in my life when I have watched wildlife with other people, when it has been a shared experience, one that may even have helped me forge a lasting connection with others. But it is very often the solitary encounters that stand out strongest in memory. They have an intensity that is diluted by company. It may in part be that wildlife is less threatened by the solitary intruder into their domain, but I think that mostly the difference takes place in my head, that I am able to engage with the wild personally rather than socially; one to one, head to head, heart to heart.

The clear cloudless skies that had made the late afternoon so exceptionally warm had the opposite effect once darkness fell. It quickly became bracingly cold, and there would certainly be an overnight frost. Stags began to roar in the nearby hills. I went inside briefly to prepare a driftwood fire. Outside again, the sky was already thick with stars. There was no moon at all, but this was the starriest sky I had seen in years, and the three of us stood with our heads tipped back, looking up. Though I had not sought it, once again I had fallen into good company.

A deer bellowed from close by, startlingly loud. I could just make out the rump of a deer not twenty feet away. I had no light, of course, but my two companions had top-of-the-range high-powered head torches. I had assumed that the deer would immediately flee from such brightness, but they seemed not to be concerned at all by the sudden blast of light. They looked up without flinching, and then continued grazing. There was a solitary stag with a dozen hinds, a couple of them little yearlings. If I had come this close in daytime, they would have panicked and run for the hills, but here in their own domain, the rules of engagement seemed to have changed. It was as if they had no frame of reference by which they could judge us as any kind of threat, and they went about their business as if we were not there at all. The stag had his work cut out, and barely had a moment to feed. Every time one of the hinds began to drift away from the group, he would race after her, forcing her back to the herd, like a sheepdog rounding up an errant lamb, nudging her in the rump with his nose. Then he would throw back his head to the stars and give a full-throated bellow that echoed through the night, and would be answered by distant stags in the hills.

The grass that grew around the village on this low ridge of wind-blown shell-sand was close-cropped turf, almost like a lawn, like the grass that grows around a rabbit warren. I presumed that the deer must come here every night, that this was the choicest grazing, with grass far sweeter than the acidic tussocks of coarse grass up on the moors. My companions and I retreated from the eye-watering cold and went to sit by the log fire and share stories. You may think of this book as being a tale told round a campfire. I could talk all night, if there was someone who wanted to hear, until the sun rose over the eastern hills. I could start all over again, on another night, by another fire, and tell a completely different set of stories, excavate a whole new set of memories. There are so many stories in a life, and so little time in which to tell them.

As the evening wore on the answering calls of the stags grew closer, and shadows passed right by the window in the candlelight. As the calls grew still louder, we headed out again. The deer were huddled around us in the darkness, grazing right up to the bothy, butting their heads against its walls. We could hear their breathing. My companions switched on their head torches. Dozens upon dozens of eyes looked up and shone back at us, but again, without flinching at all. In every direction that we could see, as far as the light reached there were deer; we were in the dead centre of a huge gathering of them.

It reminded me of a time long ago. Of course it does, you say, everything reminds him of something else. Hitching across Australia, and running low on funds, I decided to stop off in South Australia for the fruit-picking season. I set up camp on a site in the heart of the wine region, and watched as it slowly filled with trailer-dwelling seasonal workers, like something out of Steinbeck's *The Grapes of Wrath*. The vines were not yet fully ripened, so I passed a couple of weeks as I waited picking pears. Tree fruits are not particularly good earners, but at least I wasn't picking peaches. You could always spot someone immediately who had spent a day working the peaches; they would return to the campsite ash-grey and with a thousand-yard stare, and would walk like a zombie straight to the shower block. The peach fuzz got everywhere, no clothes could protect against it, and it was insanely itchy. Then the grapes ripened, and I started to make good money. I was used to piece-work and had the knack of it; not just the physical knack but the mental knack. The trick is in your focus on the job at hand; not to let your mind begin to wander, for it can make you slow down without even realising it. I took pride in trying to be the best earner on any field I was put on. The days began before light. The idea was to be on the field waiting for the very first moment it was light enough to see the bunches of grapes. We worked with a bucket of water into which we repeatedly dipped our T-shirts, for by mid-afternoon the temperature would hit the hundreds and work would be called off for the remainder of the day.

When the season was over I indulged myself with a trip out to Kangaroo Island, a good-sized island about a hundred miles long off the coast of South Australia. Much of the island is untamed bush held as a nature reserve. The wildlife of Australia is strikingly alien to that found almost anywhere else in the world, and there was much that I was hoping to see for the first time: echidnas and platypuses and koalas among them. I also hoped to see the penguins. There was a beach where a large colony of little penguins roosted each night, coming ashore at sunset after a day spent fishing out at sea. I had never seen a penguin in the wild.

I hitched to the beach with a companion, and we sat on the shore and waited. There was no sign of life, no penguins out on the water. The sun set over the sea, and not a penguin in sight. It grew dark, and still nothing. So we unrolled our sleeping bags on the rocks, and went to sleep. In the middle of the night, my companion shook me awake. She'd heard something. I sat up in the darkness. She was right, there was a kind of low muttering. It would never have been enough to wake me. I fumbled around in my pack for a torch, and switched it on. We were surrounded by a circle of penguins, just a few feet away, all facing in at us. I raised the torch beam higher, and thousands of eyes shone back at us. The entire beach was completely covered with penguins, huddled together shoulder to shoulder, every one of them staring straight at us. The only patch of beach unoccupied by penguins was the few square feet where we lay. I switched off the torch, rolled over, and went back to sleep.

In the morning when we woke at first light the beach was entirely deserted. It was hard to believe that we hadn't dreamt up these penguins. We strolled the beach looking for evidence, and finally found a solitary late riser, one little penguin hiding under a rock looking like a stuffed toy abandoned by a child. Actually, it didn't remind me of a generic stuffed toy, but of a particular straw-stuffed penguin that I'd had as an infant, from which I had been inseparable. I wonder if that ragged penguin, just about the same size as this little fellow under a rock, had been the trigger for my childhood obsession with birds and animals, which became apparent from the moment I had the words to express it. Perhaps it had been a comfort to me through those unremembered childhood illnesses that left me half-deaf.

I have been delving into my past with this journey, putting memories into words, until I have finally reached a point before memory, before words. There is nowhere else left to go from here. Memories are like pieces of a jigsaw puzzle; the completed puzzle is a whole life. If I found enough pieces I could begin to join them together, to assemble an entire life out of memory, but I suspect it would take longer to complete than to live it.

It was early when I woke beside the cold ashes of the fire, and there was no sound from the others, away in another room, so I rose and crept out for the dawn. It was light enough and I had perhaps nearly an hour before sunrise. I made my way down to the beach. The air was still now and chill, with a wintry nip in every breath, and the sky was perfectly clear and cloudless; not like the other days of this visit when the morning had always started off cloudy. I christened the sands; every footprint from yesterday had been washed away during the night. Reaching the rocks at the edge of the bay, I began to pick my way around them, staying close to the water's edge. Sometimes the ledge I was following faded away and I would reach an impasse, a low cliff, and would have to backtrack, pick another route, or cut inland over a ridge. Veins of quartz ran through the grey slabs of rock, meandering like a river seen from the sky. These rivers of crystal were things of exquisite beauty, though it would be easy to pass them by unnoticed. I pulled out my phone to take a photo; there was just enough charge left. My cameraphone had been no use for trying to take pictures of wildlife, but it was good for close-ups, and for landscapes. I scrolled through my record of the past year's wanderings. There were tight shots of autumn leaves and lichens, of seashells and birds' eggs and the footprints of birds on the beach and wildcats in the hills. There were landscapes of rocky shores, of sunrises and sunsets, of lochs and islands, of pine woods and snow-capped mountains. There were no people in these shots, and certainly no pictures of myself. There were a few shots of bothies and ruined crofts and old trails, but no contemporary houses or roads; I had been inspired to preserve a landscape with no visible trace of human existence. As with photography, so with writing. I cannot write everything, and so the process of pinning things down with words becomes as much a process of exclusion as of inclusion. My inclination had always been to seek out the natural world, to hunt for what remains of the wild and to focus on that. I had been looking for the last wilderness, and had found it, even if it had largely been a wilderness of my own mind.

On the slopes that rose from the shore were dense stands of bracken, brown and dying now, but not yet collapsed for the winter. There were little copses of coastal oak, wild and untouched, wizened and battered, still hanging on to their leaves, though they were useless now. It was still strange to see what looked like giant oaks but in miniature form; they distorted the sense of scale and proportion.

Sometimes I think that I would just like to stop; to give up on the constant roaming, the wandering, the reflecting on the past, the dwelling on the future. To say that enough is enough; enough with the restlessness, the forever wondering what is over the next horizon. To pick a place and say that this will be perfect, everything I need is here. I will just sit down and never get up; instead of going out into the world I will let the world come to me, and see what it brings. I will wait and watch the world turn about me; I will sit in silence and let silence fall. It will be a place of rest, a place where I learn to finally appreciate what is there rather than being fixated on what is missing. And when I think of choosing a place to stop in, I think of one that looks very much like this: a rocky windblown shore, mountains and sky, woods and water. These are the basic elements of what I really need.

The end of my journey was fast approaching. In the next few days I would return home, and my year of exploring the Rough Bounds would be over. I never did get to see my wildcat – although I liked to think that my wildcat saw me – and this was a good thing, I told myself, for it gave me a very good reason to return. I would spend the winter with my daughters, resting, and hopefully returning to full health, while I considered my future. Perhaps I would get my hearing tested; if nothing else, then I would at least get a number that would tell me the exact frequency at which my hearing fell off a cliff. I might be offered a hearing aid, for although my past experience with them has not been encouraging, I am told that the technology is constantly evolving. I doubted there was any way of getting my birds back, although the truth was they had never quite left me. If I closed my eyes and concentrated, I could just about make out the echo of them preserved in memory; the piercing call of a sandpiper on a mountain river, the endlessly repeated descending trill of a willow warbler in a spring wood, the winter wren suddenly breaking the silence of a frosty morning.

There was a scatter of islands; I crossed between wet, weedy rocks to a tidal island, simply because I could. It covered perhaps an acre and held a few scattered trees and a rocky peak that made it almost as high as it was wide. On its far side, facing out to sea, was its own hidden coast. I found myself on a rock that dropped straight down into deep water and a churning forest of kelp, just a few feet beneath me, and looked out. Soon the sun would rise. I stood there and waited. And then the otters came.

There was a pair of them: a mother and cub, as before. They were following the shoreline just a little way out from the water's edge, coming closer with each dive. As I had seen much further off in the bay by the little bothy on the crags, the cub was mirroring its mother's dive, following her down a moment after she disappeared. This cub had mastered the art of the dive; surfacing, not so much. While the adult would rise smoothly and gracefully for air, the cub had no patience at all. It would burst back into the light, bobbing up like a cork, rising so fast that almost its entire body cleared the water, and then it would crash back down with an untidy splash. It was learning the ropes, though; on one occasion it emerged with a cockle held between its front paws like a squirrel holding a nut, and juggled with it and nibbled at it inquisitively.

They came nearer and nearer, following a path that would take them right beneath me. There were not many times that I had been so close to wild otters. I remained motionless, but surely they must have seen me standing on my rock just above their heads. Perhaps because I was on land and they were in the water they sensed no conceivable threat. Finally, after another dive, the cub burst out of the water right beneath my feet, so close that it felt as though I could almost have reached down and stroked it. Until now, the mother had risen first and the cub had followed straight after, but this time the mother stayed down for a moment longer. The cub seemed shocked to find itself alone. It jerked its head to left and right, its panic rising, and it began to call plaintively for its mother. I could see its little mouth opening and closing; if otters had lips I would have seen it pursing them to whistle. And yet I could hear absolutely nothing at all. The mother rose gracefully a few feet away, and the baby otter streamed through the water and threw itself at her, nuzzling her and wrapping itself around her, as if they had been parted for hours. Its sheer savage joy was palpable, and I could not help but feel it too.

Dawn was fast approaching. Soon the sun would emerge above the mountain peaks across the loch. The high tops above me were already touched by light. I decided to climb the hillside, to meet the sun. I waded up through bracken and tussocks of yellow grass and into the scattered woods, then paused and looked back down at the panorama of the loch. There must have been an unseen cleft in the mountains across the bay, for the light first appeared at right angles to me. A misty green ray of light appeared from the midst of the hills and swept down the mountainside opposite, then bathed the waters of the loch in a pale radiance, like the beam of a lighthouse slowly turning. I could feel the world moving beneath my feet, unstoppable, irrepressible. Above me the hillside was bathed in golden sunshine, in a long horizontal band that crept ever closer, moment by moment. I struck out for the hills, walking into the light.

Acknowledgements

My thanks always are due to my agent, Jessica Woollard at David Higham Associates. Without you, I suspect I might not have a career, or not this one, at any rate.

My appreciation also to my editor, Imogen Taylor, who helped make this book's slow march from idea to reality such a smooth and enjoyable process, and to Amy Perkins and the rest of the team at The Tinder Press and at Headline. Writing may be a solitary affair, but producing a book is a team effort, involving many people whose names I don't know doing jobs that I don't understand, and they seldom get the recognition they deserve.

During my travels in Scotland I crossed paths, sometimes literally, with many people, some of whom found a brief mention in this book. I have also at times referred glancingly to my companions on those earlier journeys that I have recollected in these pages. If I have not done you justice, I hope you will accept that it is not because I think your stories are not worth telling, but rather out of discretion, and feeling that your own stories are not really mine to tell. My thanks to you all.

To my mother Jean, my first and least critical reader, my eternal thanks for a lifetime of support and encouragement, and to my daughters Kaya and Anya, my thanks for putting up with my occasional absences and the distractedness that sometimes comes from being lost in words, and for generally making life fun.